Mystic Shawls 2

Anna Dalvi

Cooperative Press
Cleveland, Ohio

Mystic Shawls

ISBN 13 (print): 978-1-937513-83-2
ISBN 13 (e-book): 978-1-937513-84-9
First Edition
Published by Cooperative Press
http://www.cooperativepress.com

Patterns © 2017, Anna Dalvi
Photos © 2017, Crissy Jarvis
Model: Madison Newey

Every effort has been made to ensure that all the information in this book is accurate at the time of publication; however, Cooperative Press neither endorses nor guarantees the content of external links referenced in this book.

If you have questions or comments about this book, or need information about licensing, custom editions, special sales, or academic/corporate purchases, please contact

Cooperative Press: info@cooperativepress.com or 10252 Berea Rd, Cleveland, OH 44102 USA

No part of this book may be reproduced in any form, except brief excerpts for the purpose of review, without prior written permission of the publisher. Thank you for respecting our copyright.

For Cooperative Press
Senior Editor: Shannon Okey
Layout Editor: Kim Saar
Series Book Designer: Kayt de Fever

To Aneesh
and to Linnea, Axel & Viggo
Thanks for always cheering me on!

contents

Mystic Supernova 9	Mystic Ocean 15	Mystic Vortex 21	Mystic Cuppa 31
Mystic Cabin 37	Mystic Junction 47	Mystic Sea Witch 55	Mystic Haven 63
Mystic Sunset 71	Mystic Mist 75	Zorya 81	Dažbog 89

Abbreviations
&
Symbol Guide

introduction

I love lace. And I love designing lace shawls. I love the idea of starting with a blank "canvas" for explorations in lace patterns and colors.

All of the patterns in *Mystic Shawls 2* were originally published as mystery knitalongs. This means that the patterns have been released in weekly instalments and that the knitters only had a vague idea of what the finished shawl would be like. The theme and shape are known to the knitters up front, but no one has seen the finished piece when they start to knit it.

Patterns for mystery knitalongs are a special challenge to design, because I aim to make every clue a little bit different from the previous clues, so it's not so obvious how the pattern will develop. And yet, they do have to have a cohesive look when completed, so they do not look like a random collection of stitch patterns. The design process is a fun challenge, almost like solving a puzzle.

Many of the shawls in this book have been designed using either gradient yarn or multiple colors. In a few cases, the gradients have been used in more unusual ways. For example, Mystic Haven is worked from both ends of a gradient skein, to emphasize the contrast between the two end colors. Mystic Cabin, on the other hand, uses the colors "out of order". And Mystic Sunset uses a contrast color to break up the gradient, but still works the gradient colors in order to give the illusion of a fade.

When I design shawls, I generally start by working out the shape of the shawl. I figure out where to place the increases and/or decreases that creates the desired shape. This then forms my "canvas" that has to be filled with patterns and colors. The lace patterns and the colors are selected to work with the theme of the shawl. For example, Mystic Cabin is a play on the popular log cabin blankets. I stacked "logs" made out of lace and garter stitch panels, to form a triangular shawl. And of course I had to use a color reminiscent of the cedar logs of our cottage. The Mystic Mist colors were selected because they look like the sun breaking through the morning mist - golden oranges in the centre, dissolving into misty grey on the outer edges. Mystic Ocean uses sea-foam greens, and Mystic Haven started with the idea of a safe Robin's nest.

The last two shawls in the book—Zorya and Dažbog—were designed as Advent KALendars. Just like chocolate advent calendars contain a daily treat for the 24 days leading up to Christmas, so do these knitters' KALendars. For each day there is a new a small part of the pattern, and by the end of the KALendar you will have completed a brand new lace shawl. In the book, you will see that the Advent KALendar patterns are still presented in twenty-four pieces, one for each day.

I hope you'll enjoy knitting these shawls as much as I have. And even though my design inspiration often involves the colors chosen, I encourage you to make the shawl YOURS by selecting colors that speak to you.

Happy knitting!

mystic supernova

Mystic Supernova is a circular shawl inspired by the stellar explosions that are so bright they can outshine an entire galaxy. It starts with a small star in the center and grows outwards.

Mystic Supernova

MATERIALS

1 skein Lace-Garn from Wollmeise [100% merino – 1740 yds/1591 m per 300 g] in *Terra di Siena*

3.75 mm [US 5] needles

Stitch markers

Large-eyed, blunt needle

GAUGE

15 sts and 11 rows = 10 cm [4 in] in pattern, blocked

FINISHED (BLOCKED) SIZE

Diameter: 183 cm [72 in]

CIRCULAR SHAWL INSTRUCTIONS

CO 9 sts using invisible loop.

Divide evenly on 3 DPNs (switch to circular needles when you have enough stitches on the needles, or use magic loop).

Rnd 1: K9, place a marker to mark the beginning of the rnds.
Rnd 2: [K1, yo] repeat 9 times. (18 sts)
Rnd 3–5: Knit.
Rnd 6: [K1, yo] repeat 18 times. (36 sts)
Rnd 7–12: Knit.
Rnd 13: [K1,yo] repeat 36 times. (72 sts)

Note: All even rnds from this point are knit.

Section 1

Work Chart A 12 times around.
Rnd 27: [K1, yo] repeat 72 times (144 sts)
Rnd 28: Knit

Section 2

Work Chart B 12 times around.
Rnd 53: [K1, yo] repeat 144 times. (288 sts)
Rnd 54: Knit.

Section 3

Work Chart C 12 times around.
Rnd 103: [K1, yo] repeat 288 times. (576 sts)
Rnd 104: Knit.

Section 4

Work Chart D 12 times around.

Edging

K1, break the yarn. CO 5 sts with a provisional cast on. At the end of each RS row, k2tog the last stitch of the edging with the next stitch of the shawl, starting with the next stitch on the needles (which was formerly the 2nd stitch of the round).

Work Edging Chart, working rows 1-24 FORTY-EIGHT times.

Graft rem 5 sts with the 5 sts from the provisional cast on.

FINISHING INSTRUCTIONS

Sew in ends and block.

SEMI-CIRCULAR SHAWL INSTRUCTIONS

CO 2 sts by knitting them on.

Setup row 1: Kfb, kfb. (4 sts)
Setup row 2: Kfb 4 times. (8 sts)
Setup row 3: K2, p4, k2.

All WS rows (even rows) are K2, p until 2 sts remain, k2

Row 1: K2, [yo, k1] repeat 4 times, yo, k2. (13 sts)
Row 3: K13.
Row 5: K2, [k1, yo] repeat 9 times, k2. (22 sts)
Row 7: K22.
Row 9–12: as rows 7-8.
Row 13: K2, [k1,yo] repeat 18 times, k2. (40 sts)

Note: all even rows from this point are K2, p to the last 2 stitches, k2.

Section 1

RS rows: K2, [Chart A] 6 times, k2.
Row 27: k2, [k1, yo] repeat 36 times, k2. (76 sts)
Row 28: k2, p72, k2.

Section 2

RS rows: K2, [Chart B] 6 times, k2.
Row 53: k2, [k1, yo] repeat 72 times, k2. (148 sts)
Row 54: k2, p144, k2.

Section 3

RS rows: K2, [Chart C] 6 times, k2.
Row 103: k2, [k1, yo] repeat 144 times, k2. (292 sts)
Row 104: k2, p288, k2.

Section 4

RS rows: K2, [Chart D] 6 times, k2.

Edging

CO 5 sts with a knit cast on.

Set-up Row 1 (RS): K4, k2tog last st with first st on the body of the shawl.
et-up Row 2 (WS): Sl1, purl to last 2 sts, k2.
Work set-up rows 1-2 twice more, then work Edging Chart.

Work Edging Chart, working rows 1-24 TWENTY-THREE times. Then work rows 1-22 once more.

Finish edging:

Row 1 (RS): K3, k2tog, k2tog last st with the next st on the body of the shawl.
Row 2 (WS): Sl1, purl to last 2 sts, k2.
Row 3 (RS): K4, k2tog last st with the next st on the body of the shawl.
Row 4: as row 2.

BO as follows: K2, *return to ln, k2tog tbl, k1, rep from * until no unworked sts remain.

FINISHING

Sew in ends and block.

Mystic Supernova – CHART A

Mystic Supernova – CHART B

Mystic Supernova – CHART C

Mystic Supernova – CHART D

Mystic Supernova – EDGING

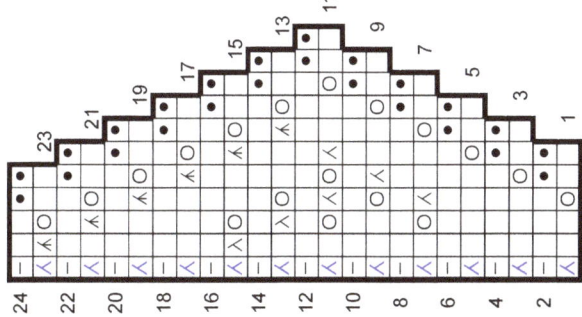

mystic ocean

Imagine the vast ocean—rolling waves, thundering waves, and masses of water. It can be violent or entirely calm and peaceful, intimidating dark gray or brilliant turquoise. You could find yourself sailing on the surface of the ocean, or plunging deep down into its never-ending depths.

Mystic Ocean

MATERIALS

1 Gradient Set (Set of 5 Yummy 2-ply Toes) from MissBabs [100% merino wool – 665 yds/608 m per 6.5 oz] in *Aquarius*

4.0 mm [US 6] needles

Stitch markers

Large-eyed, blunt needle

GAUGE

14 sts and 28 rows = 4 in [10 cm] in pattern, blocked

FINISHED (BLOCKED) SIZE

Wingspan: 214 cm [84"], height: 46 cm [18"]

INSTRUCTIONS

This shawl can be knit lightest to darkest, or vice versa. Your choice. My sample is lightest to darkest.

With [C1] CO 7 sts.
Set-up Row 1 (WS): K7.

Chart A

With [C1] work Rows 1-20. Then work rows 9-20 THREE more times, each time adding 6 repeats of the stitches in the box. (173 sts)

Chart B

With [C2] work rows 57-70. (215 sts)

Chart C

With [C2] work rows 71-82. (251 sts)

Chart D

With [C3] work rows 83-94. (287 sts)

Chart E

With [C3] work rows 95-100.
With [C4] work rows 101-108. (329 sts)

Chart F

With [C4] work rows 109-118.
With [C5] work rows 119-120. (365 sts)

Chart G

With [C5] work rows 121-130. (389 sts)

FINISHING INSTRUCTIONS

Row 131-132: Knit.

Then bind off as follows: K2, *return to left needle, k2tog through back loop, k1, repeat from * until no unworked stitches remain.

Sew in ends and block. When blocking, pull out the center stitches of the ⑪ to points.

Mystic Ocean – CHART A

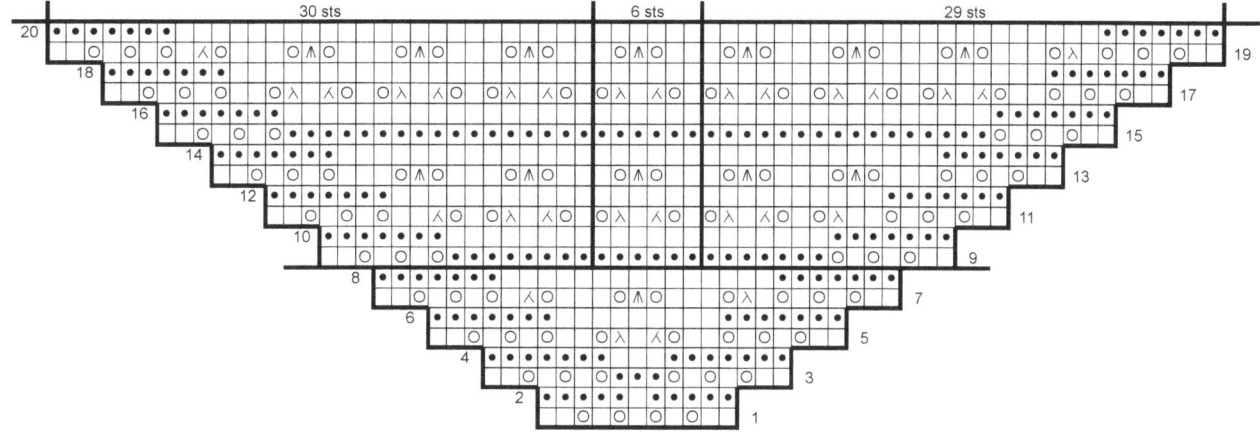

Mystic Ocean – CHART B

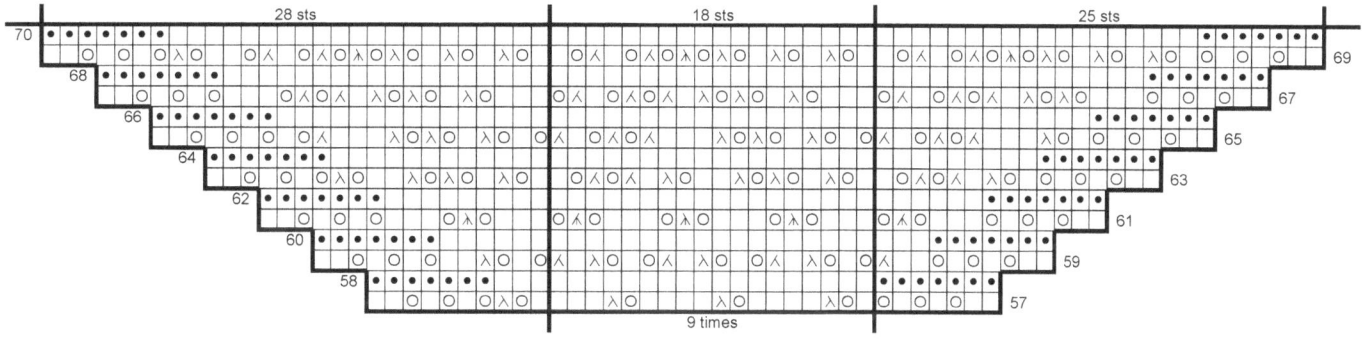

Mystic Ocean – CHART C

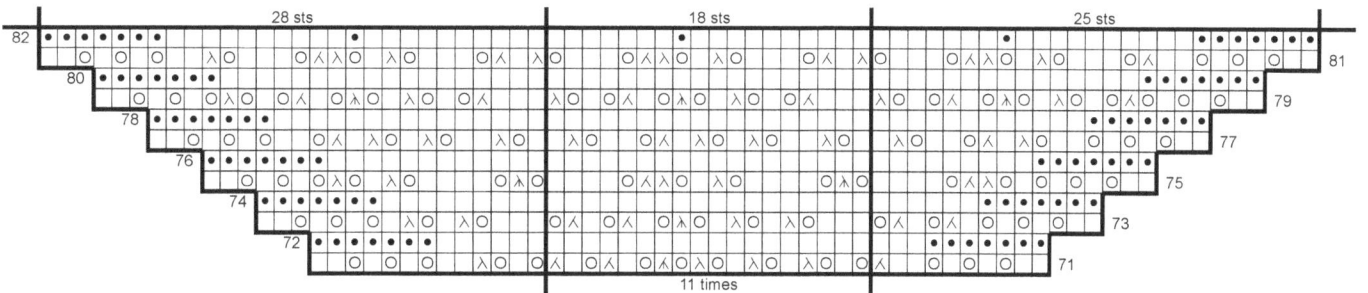

Mystic Ocean – CHART D

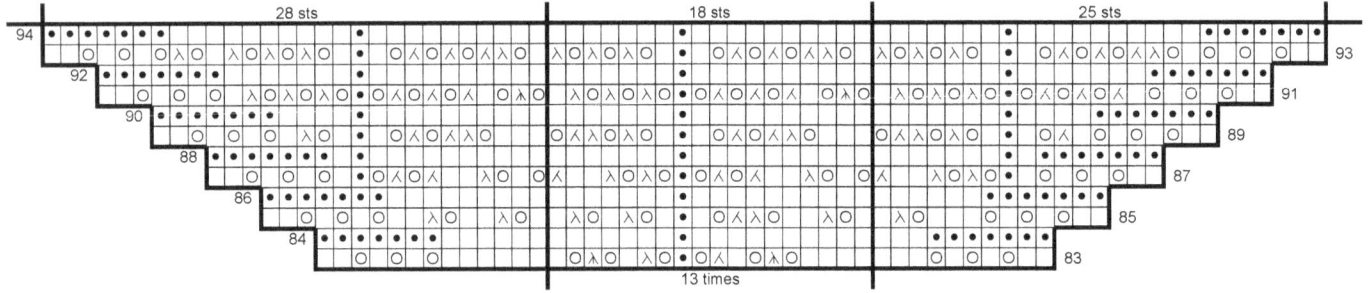

Mystic Ocean – CHART E

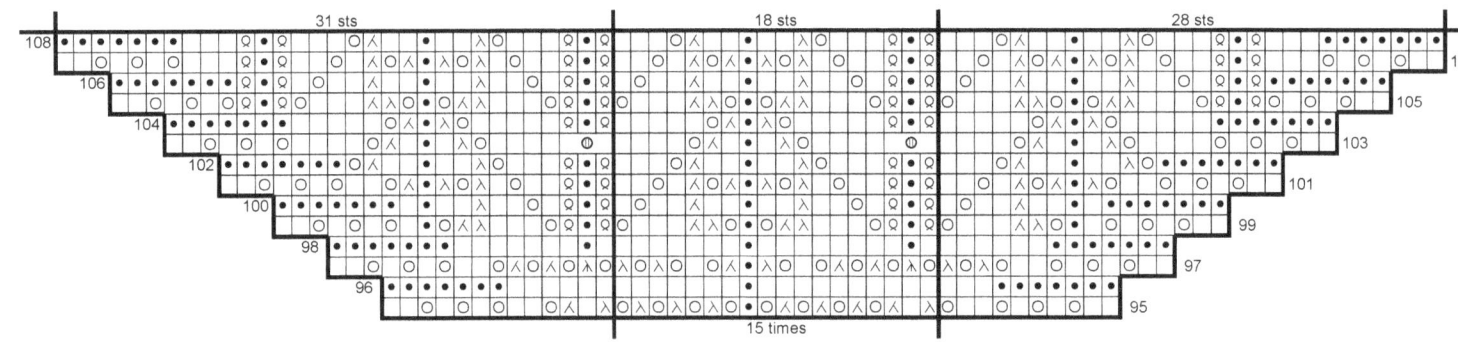

Mystic Ocean – CHART F

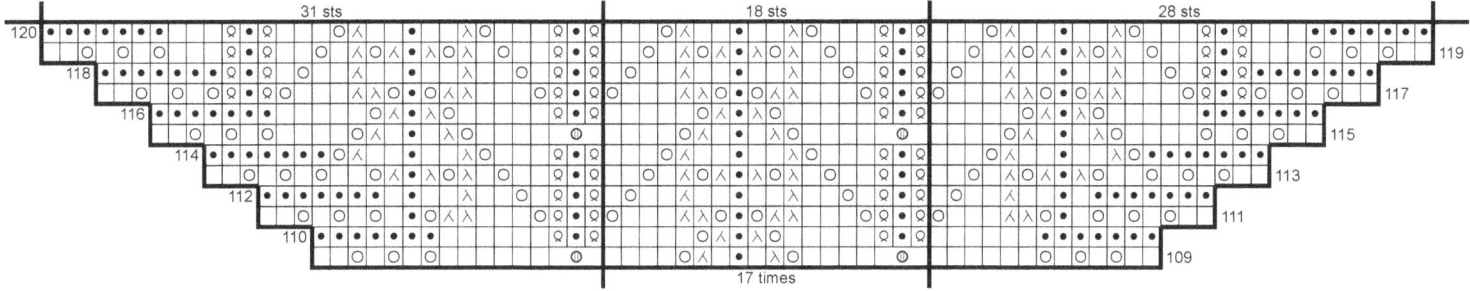

Mystic Ocean – CHART G

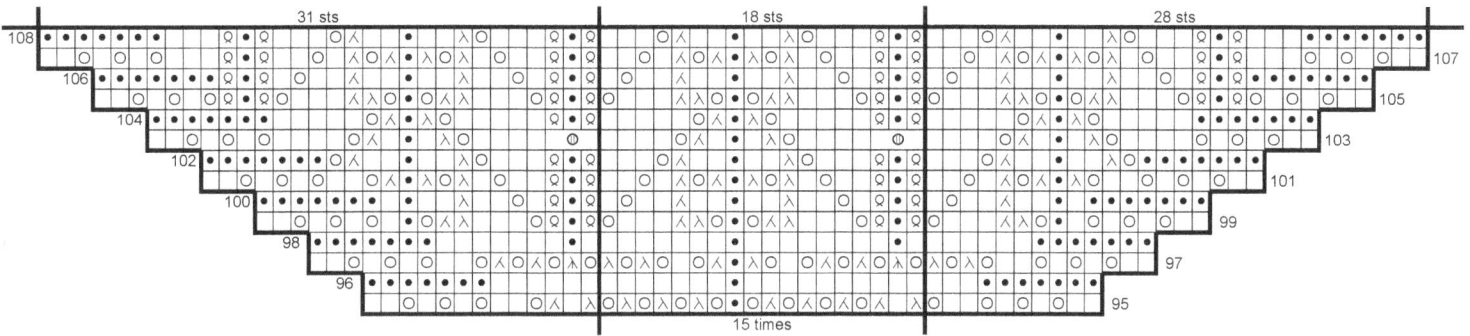

mystic vortex

Mystic Vortex started with the idea of a swirling vortex, and capturing the sense of movement in a lace pattern.

Mystic Vortex

MATERIALS

1 or 2 Lace Paintbox Gradients from Fiber Optic Yarns [100% merino wool – 900 yds/823 m per 3.6 oz] in *Damson-Gold Gradient*

3.75 mm [US 5] needles

Stitch markers

Large-eyed, blunt needle

Mystic Vortex can be knit as a circular shawl (1,800 yds lace weight yarn) or a semicircular shawl (900 yds lace weight yarn).

GAUGE

20 sts and 38 rows = 4 in [10 cm] in stockinette stitch, blocked

FINISHED (BLOCKED) SIZE

Diameter: 160 cm [63 in]

CIRCULAR SHAWL INSTRUCTIONS

CO 9 sts using invisible loop.

Divide evenly on 3 DPNs (switch to circular needles when you have enough stitches on the needles, or use magic loop).

Rnd 1: K9, place a marker to mark the beginning of the rnds.
Rnd 2: [K1, yo] repeat 9 times. (18 sts)
Rnd 3-5: Knit.
Rnd 6: [K1, yo] repeat 18 times. (36 sts)
Rnd 7-12: Knit.
Rnd 13: [K1,yo] repeat 36 times. (72 sts)

Section 1

Work Chart A 12 times around.

All even rnds in Section 1 are knit.

Rnd 27: [K1, yo] repeat 72 times. (144 sts)
Rnd 28: Knit.

Section 2

Work Chart B 12 times around.

All even rnds in Section 2 are knit.

nd 53: [K1, yo] repeat 144 times. (288 sts)
Rnd 54: Knit.

Section 3

Work Chart C 12 times around.

In this section, the start of Rnd will be shifted during rnds 60, 66, 72, 80, 86, 93, 98, and 102.

Even rnds are worked as follows:
Rnds 56, 58: K288.
Rnd 60: K288, RM, k3, PM.
Rnds 62, 64: K288.
Rnd 66: K288, RM, k3, PM.
Rnds 68, 70: K288.
Rnd 72: K288, RM, k3, PM.
Rnds 74, 76, 78: K288.
Rnd 80: K285, PM. (Remove old beg of rnd marker when working Rnd 81.)
Rnds 82, 84: K288.
Rnd 86: K285, PM. (Remove old beg of rnd marker when working Rnd 87.)
Rnds 88, 90: K288.

Mystic Vortex Circular – CHART A

Mystic Vortex Circular – CHART B

Rnd 92: K285, PM. (Remove old beg of rnd marker when working Rnd 93.)
Rnds 94, 96: K288.
Rnd 98: K286, PM. (Remove old beg of rnd marker when working Rnd 99.)
Rnd 102: K288, RM, k2, PM.
Rnd 103: [K1, yo] repeat 288 times. (576 sts)
Rnd 104: Knit.

Section 4

Work Chart D 12 times around.

All even rnds in Section 4 are knit.

In this section, the start of Rnd will be shifted during rnds 105, 135, and 170.

Rnd 105: RM, k14, PM, charted-row.
Rnd 135: RM, k10, PM, charted-row.
Rnd 170: K566, PM. (Remove old beg. of rnd marker when working Rnd 171.)
Rnd 200: K576, RM, k2.

Edging

Break yarn. CO 5 sts using a provisional cast-on. If using the Paintbox gradient, start the edging with the other end of the gradient. Start working the charts. After rows 24, 48, 72, and 96, turn the work and BO 10 sts as follows:

K2, (return sts to left needle, k2tog through back loop, k1) 10 times. The stitch remaining on your RN is the first □ on the chart for the next row.

Work rows 1-96 TWELVE times. After the 12th repeat, BO 10 sts as before, then Graft rem 5 sts with the 5 sts from the provisional cast on.

FINISHING INSTRUCTIONS

Bind off as follows: K2, *return 2 sts to ln, k2tog through back loop, k1, rep from * until no unworked sts remain.

Sew in ends and block.

Mystic Vortex Circular – CHART C

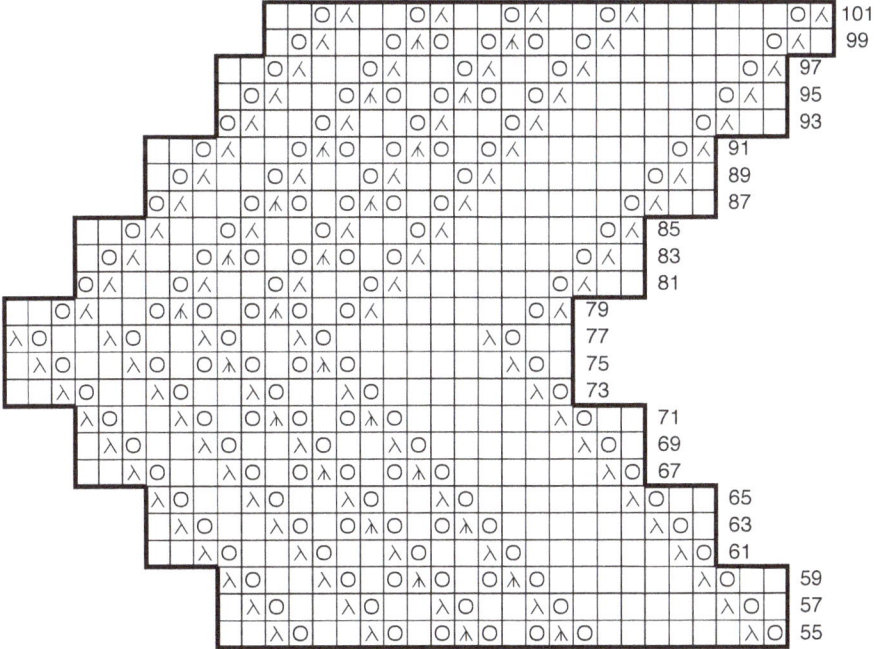

Mystic Vortex Circular – Chart D

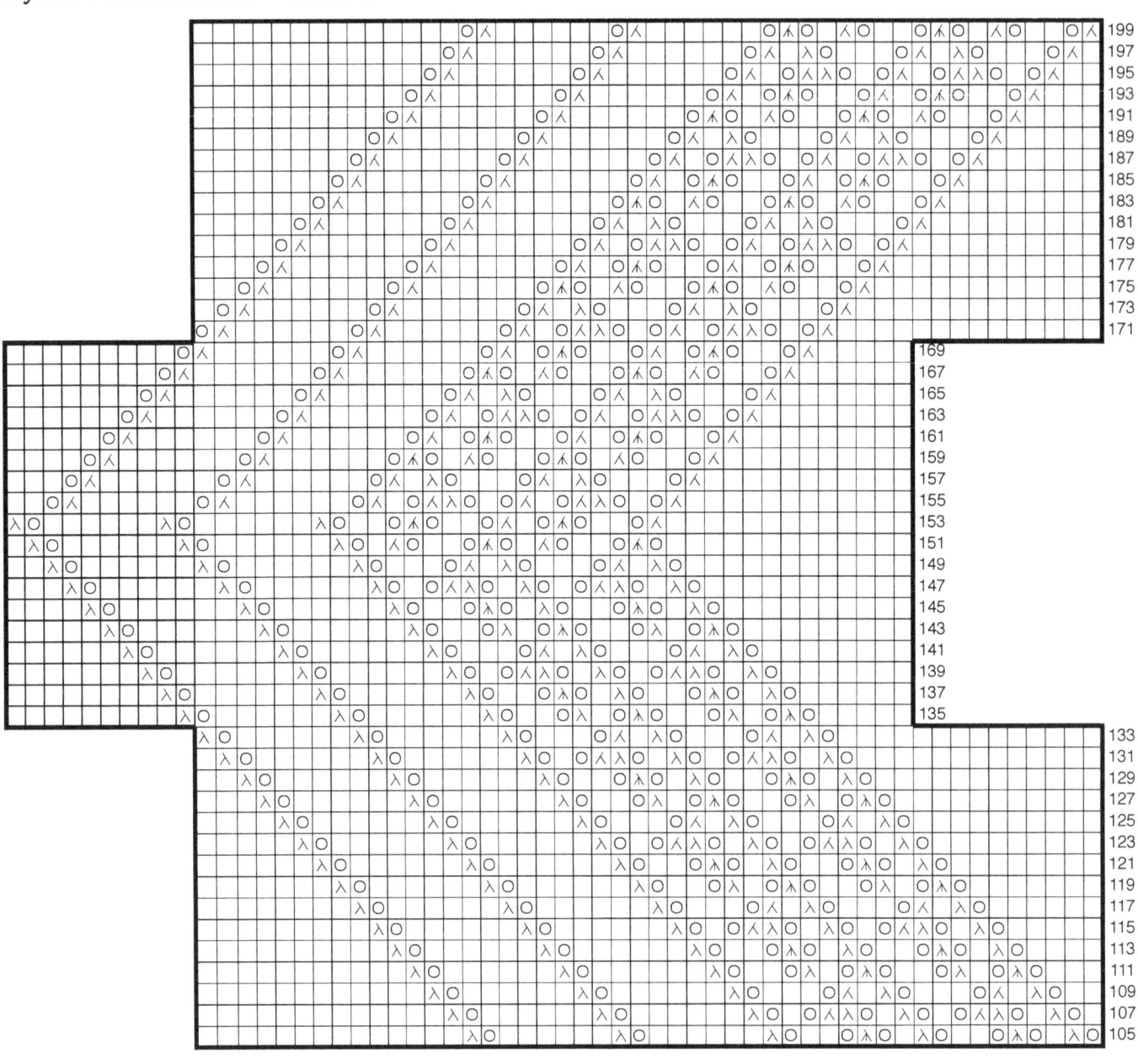

Mystic Vortex Circular – EDGING

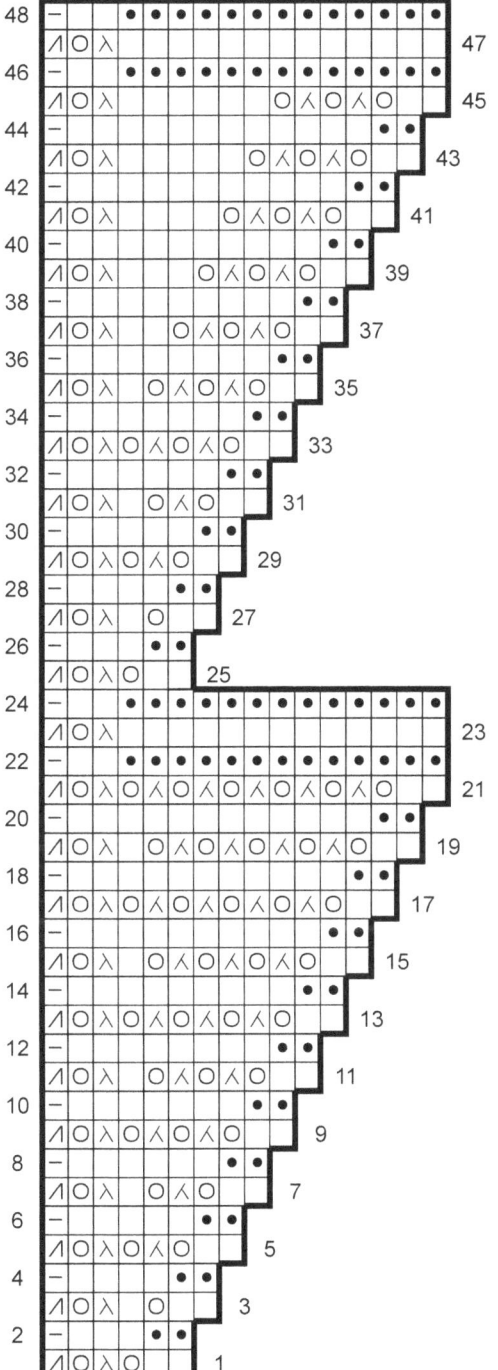
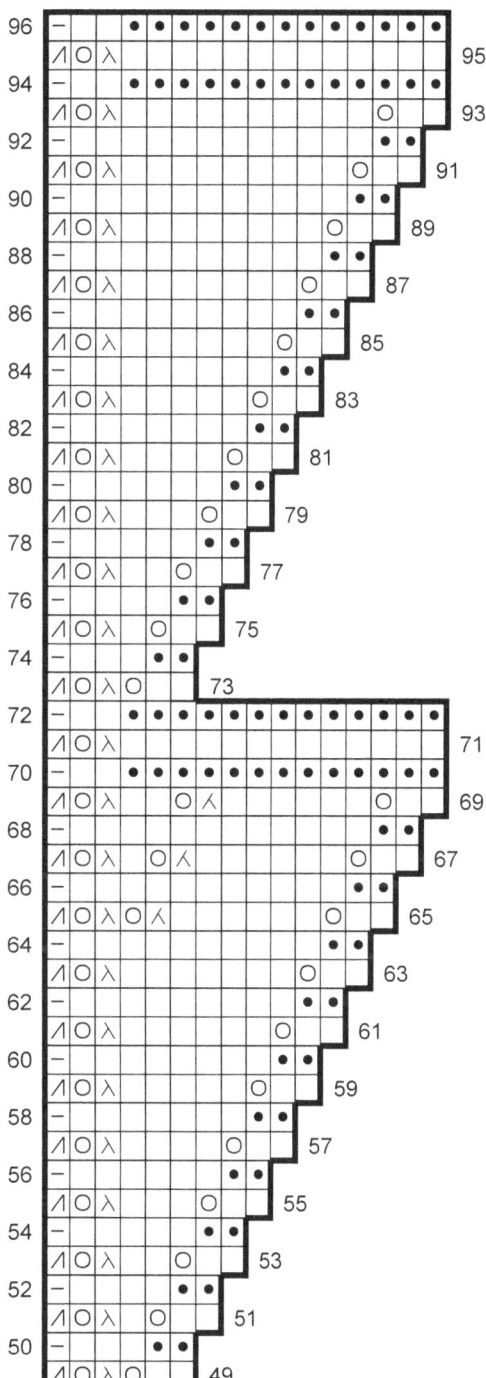

SEMI-CIRCULAR SHAWL INSTRUCTIONS

CO 2 sts by knitting them on.

Setup row 1: Kfb, kfb. (4 sts)
Setup row 2: Kfb 4 times. (8 sts)
Setup row 3: K2, p4, k2.

All WS rows (even rows) are K2, p until 2 sts remain, k2

Row 1: K2, [yo, k1] repeat 4 times, yo, k2. (13 sts)
Row 3: K13.
Row 5: K2, [k1, yo] repeat 9 times, k2. (22 sts)
Row 7: K22.
Row 9-12: as rows 7-8.
Row 13: K2, [k1,yo] repeat 18 times, k2. (40 sts)

Note: all even rows from this point are K2, p to the last 2 stitches, k2.

Section 1

Work Semi-Circular Chart A.

RS rows: [Charted Row]
Row 27: K2, [k1, yo] repeat 36 times, k2. (76 sts)
Row 28: K2, p72, k2.

Section 2

Work Semi-Circular Chart B.

RS rows: [Charted Row]
Row 53: K2, [k1, yo] repeat 72 times, k2. (148 sts)
Row 54: K2, p144, k2.

Section 3

Work Semi-Circular Chart C.

RS rows: [Charted Row]
Row 103: K2, [k1, yo] repeat 144 times, k2. (292 sts)
Row 104: K2, p288, k2.

Section 4

Work Semi-Circular Chart D.

RS rows: [Charted Row]
Row 200: K2, p to the last 2 stitches, k2.

Edging

If using the Paintbox gradient, start the edging with the other end of the gradient. CO 5 sts with a knit cast on.

Set-up Row 1 (RS): K4, k2tog last st with first st on the body of the shawl.
Set-up Row 2 (WS): Sl1, purl to last 2 sts, k2.

Work set-up rows 1-2 once more, then start working the charts.

After rows 24, 48, 72, and 96, turn the work and BO 11 sts as follows:

K2, [return sts to left needle, k2tog through back loop, k1] 11 times.

The stitch remaining on your RN is the first ☐ on the chart for the next row.

Work rows 1-96 SIX times.

Finish edging:

Row 1 (RS): K4, k2tog, k2tog last st with the next st on the body of the shawl.
Row 2 (WS): Sl1, purl to last 2 sts, k2.
Row 3 (RS): K4, k2tog last st with the next st on the body of the shawl.
Row 4: as row 2.

BO all sts.

FINISHING INSTRUCTIONS

Bind off as follows: K2, *return 2 sts to ln, k2tog through back loop, k1, rep from * until no unworked sts remain.

Sew in ends and block.

Mystic Vortex Semi-Circular – CHART A

Mystic Vortex Semi-Circular – CHART B

Mystic Vortex Semi-Circular – CHART C

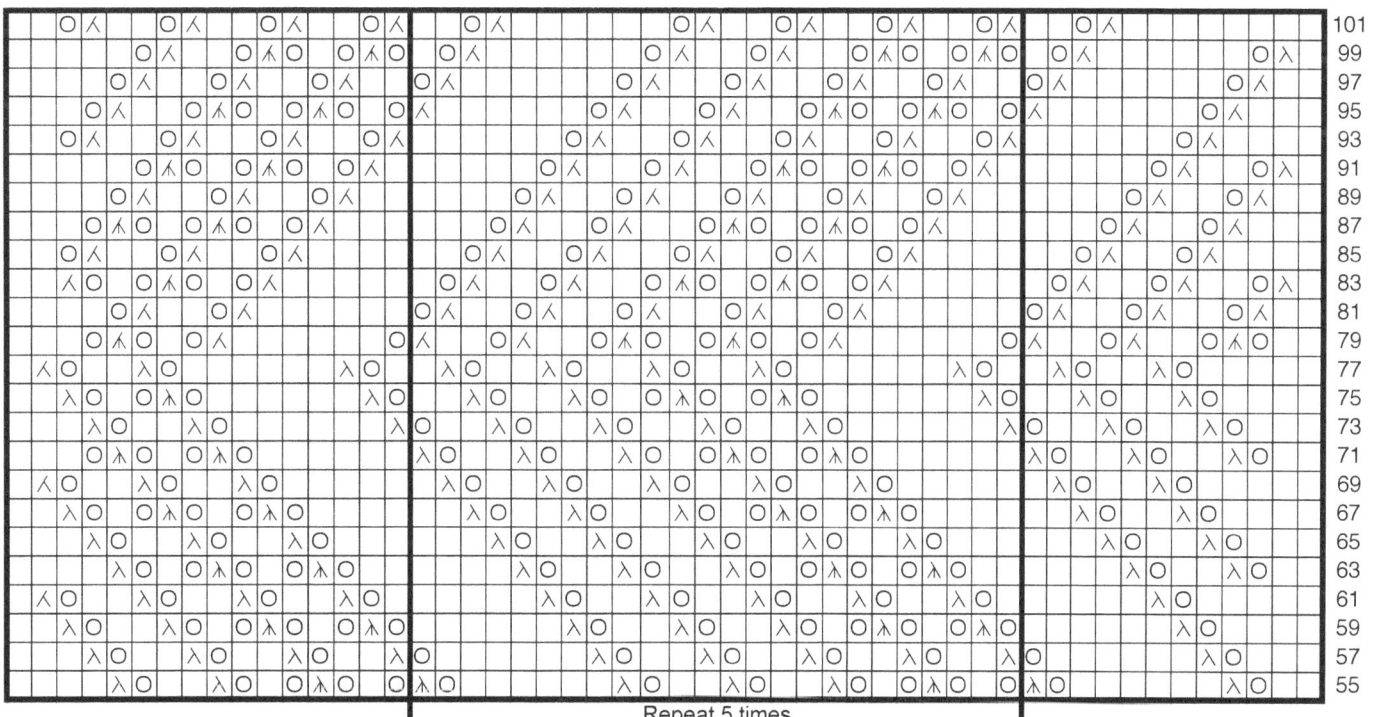

Mystic Vortex Semi-Circular – CHART D

Mystic Vortex Semi-Circular – EDGING

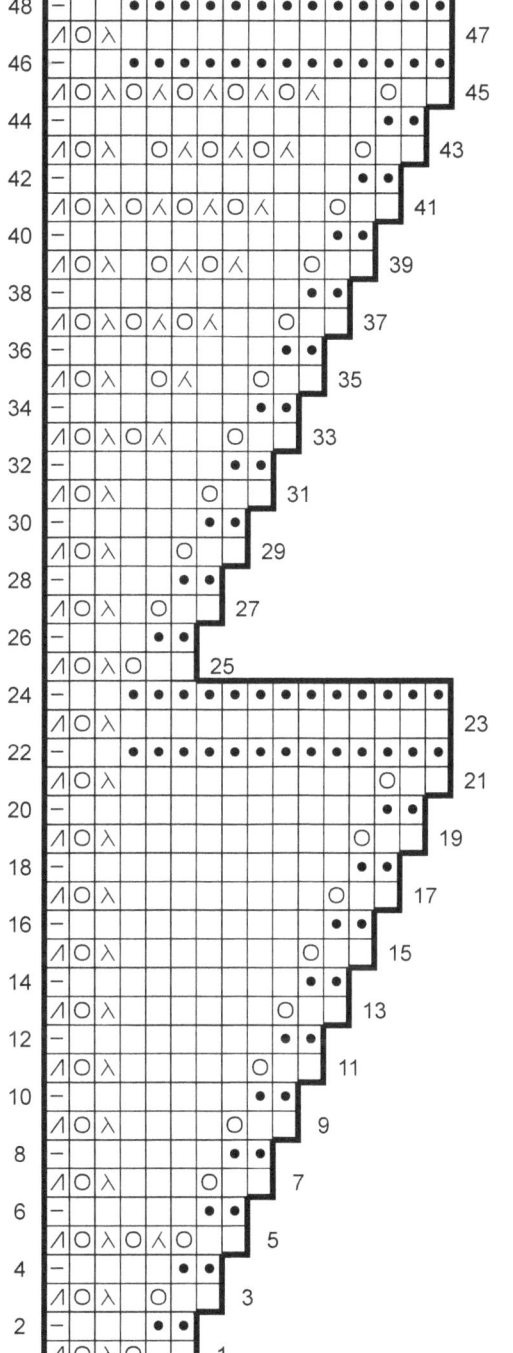
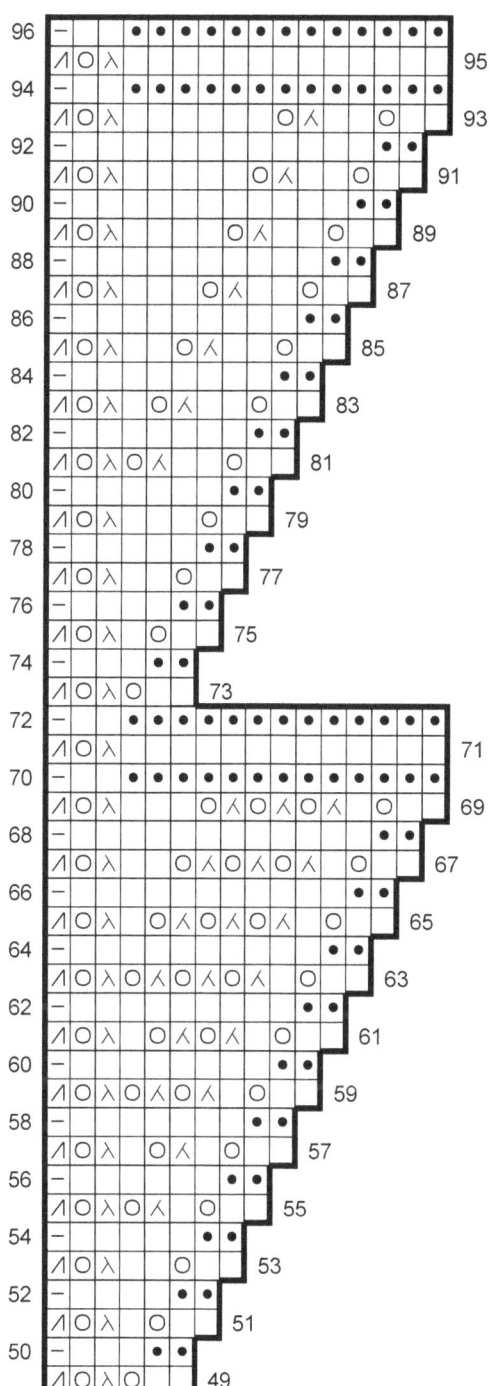

mystic cuppa

When the world is all at odds
And the mind is all at sea
Then cease the useless tedium
And brew a cup of tea.
There is magic in its fragrance,
There is solace in its taste;
And the laden moments vanish
Somehow into space.
And the world becomes a lovely thing!
There's beauty as you'll see;
All because you briefly stopped
To brew a cup of tea.

Mystic Cuppa

MATERIALS

4 skeins Bohemia Sport from Outlaw Yarn [45% Polwarth, 45% Alpaca, 10% Possum –182 yds/166 m per 50 g] in two contrasting colors (2 skeins in *earl* + 2 skeins in *carnivale*)

4.5 mm [US 7] needles

2 cable needles

Stitch markers

Large-eyed, blunt needle

GAUGE

13.5 sts and 27 rows = 10 cm [4 in] in pattern, blocked

FINISHED (BLOCKED) SIZE

Wingspan: 211 cm [83 in], height: 70 cm [27.5 in]

INSTRUCTIONS

CO 7 sts.

Set-up Row 1 (WS): K7.

The charts are color-coded; white stitches are knit on one color, gray in the other.

Cast on with the color you want to use for your white stitches on the chart.

Chart A

Work rows 1-14. Then work rows 7-14 TWO more times, each time adding 3 repeats of the stitches in the box. (113 sts)

Chart B

Work rows 37-46, working the stitches in the box 13 times.

Then work rows 39-46 TWO more times, each time adding 3 repeats of the stitches in the box. (209 sts)

Chart C

Work rows 69-78, working the stitches in the box 25 times. Then work rows 71-78 TWO more times, each time adding 3 repeats of the stitches in the box. (305 sts)

Chart D

Work Rows 101-118, working the stitches in the box 12 times. (359 sts)

Chart E

Work Rows 119-135, working the stitches in the box 14 times. (413 sts)

FINISHING INSTRUCTIONS

Row 136 (WS): K with color B
Row 137-138: K with color A.

Then bind off as follows with color A: K2, *return to left needle, k2tog through back loop, k1, repeat from * until no unworked stitches remain.

Sew in ends and block.

Mystic Cuppa – CHART A

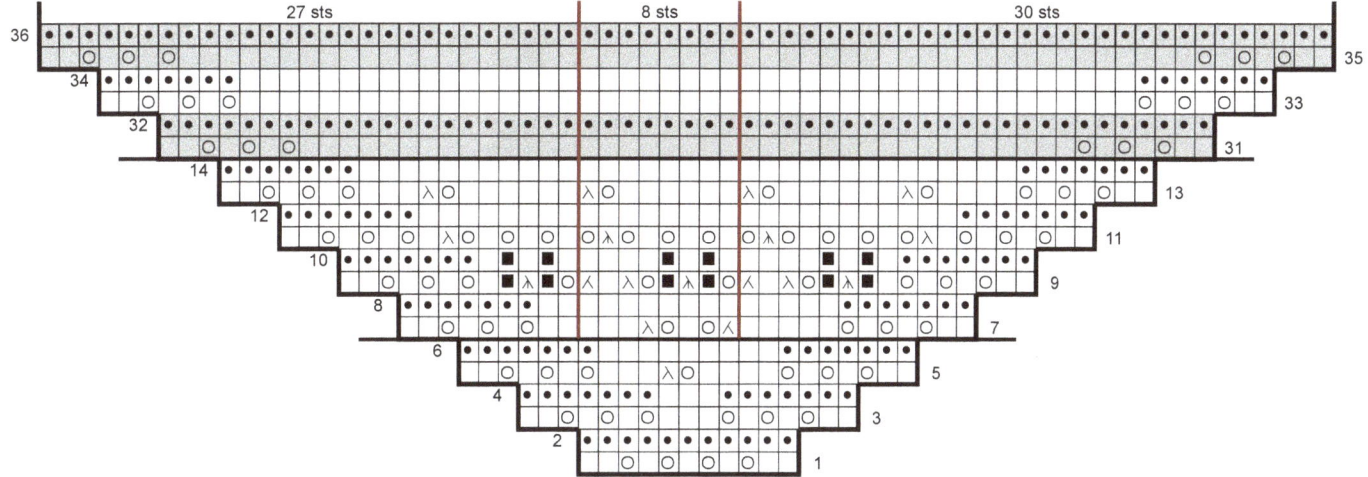

Mystic Cuppa – CHART B

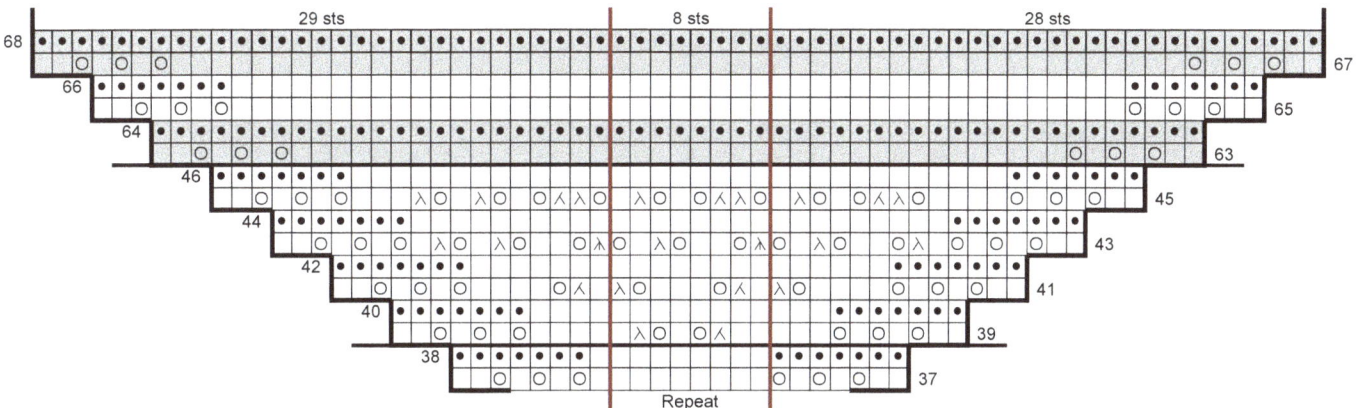

Mystic Cuppa – CHART C

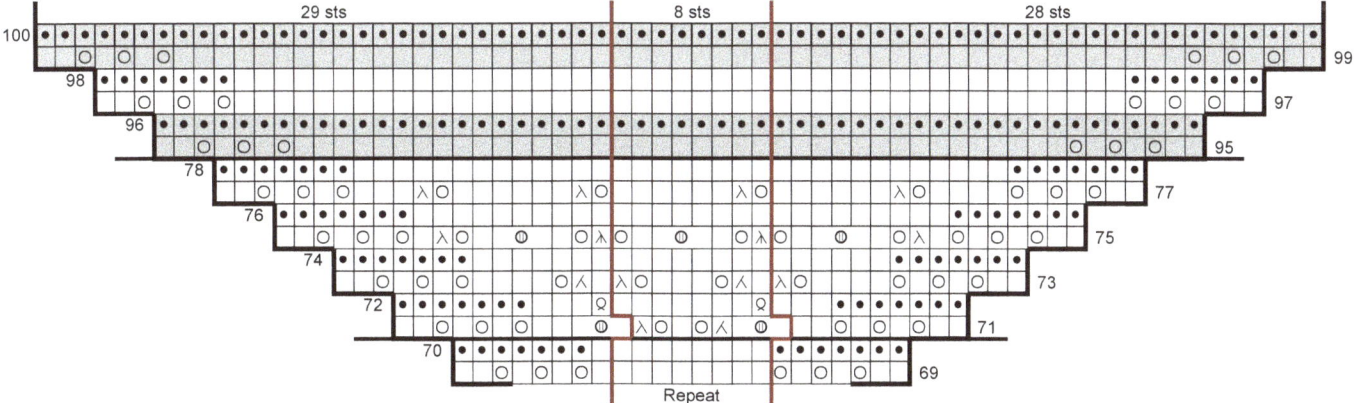

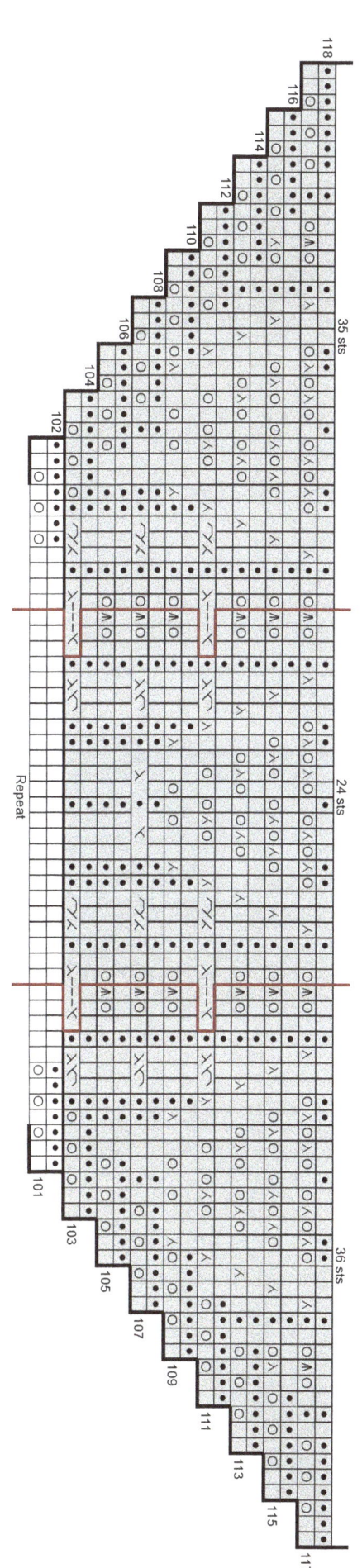

Mystic Cuppa – CHART D

Mystic Cuppa – CHART E

mystic cabin

Mystic Cabin is a cozy shawl to wrap yourself in, when a warm summer day turns into a cool summer night, and you're sitting by the camp fire, looking into the dancing flames and listening to the crackling fire.

Mystic Cabin

MATERIALS

1 gradient kit of Pebble Sock from Black Trillium Yarn (100% super wash merino, 580 m/635 yds 165 g, 5 shades of one color) or similar yarn [C1-C5] OR 2 skeins of contrasting color Pebble Sock [SC1-SC2]

3.75 mm [US 5] needles (2 sets)

Stitch markers

Large-eyed, blunt needle

GAUGE

16 sts and 32 rows = 10 cm [4 in] in garter stitch, blocked

FINISHED (BLOCKED) SIZE

Wingspan: 170 cm (67 in), height: 94 cm (37 in) adjustable in pattern

INSTRUCTIONS

SECTION 1

With [C1 or SC1], CO 3 sts using a provisional CO.

Set-up Row: K3.

Charted Instructions

Follow Chart 1.

Written Instructions

Row 1: K1, M1, k2
Row 2: Knit.
Row 3: K until 2 sts rem, M1, k2.
Row 4: Knit.

Repeat rows 3-4 nine times. (14 sts)

SECTION 2

With second set of needles and [C3 or SC2]:

Row 1 (RS): Pick up and knit 3 sts from provisional CO, then pick up and knit 12 sts (one for each purl bump) from the side of section 1 (marked in blue on the chart).

Charted Instructions

Follow Chart 2.

Written Instructions

Row 2 (WS): K1, k2tog, yo, k1, yo, ssk, k1, k2tog, yo, k1, yo, ssk, k3.

Row 3: K2, M1, ssk, yo, k3, yo, CDD, yo, k3, yo, k2tog.

Row 4: K1, yo, ssk, k1, k2tog, yo, k1, yo, ssk, k1, k2tog, yo, k4.

Row 5: K2, M1, k3, yo, CDD, yo, k3, yo, CDD, yo, k2.

Row 6: K17.

With [C2 or SC1]:
Row 7: K2, M1, k to the end.

Row 8: Knit.

Work rows 7-8 nine times. (26 sts)

Mystic Cabin – CHART 1

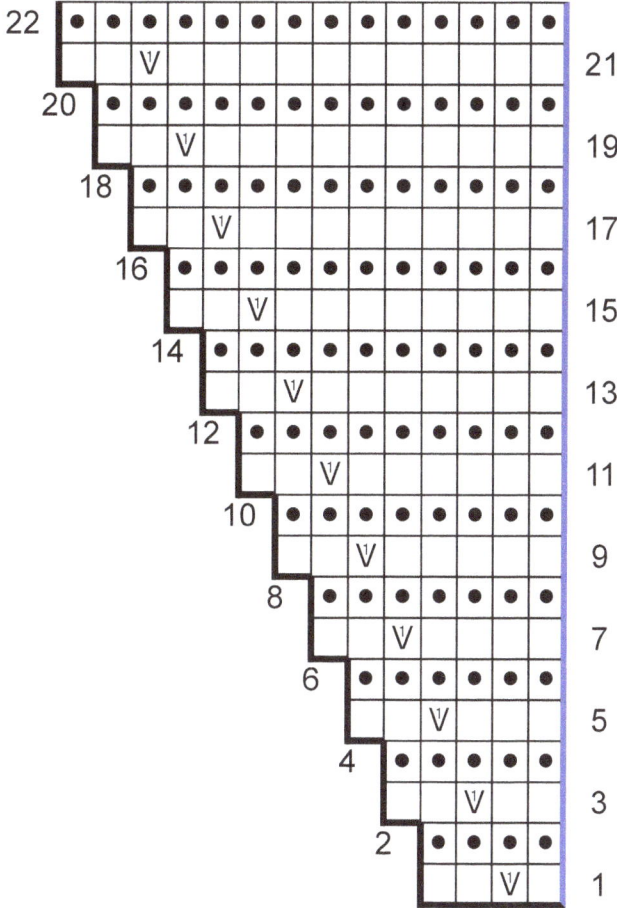

Mystic Cabin – CHART 2

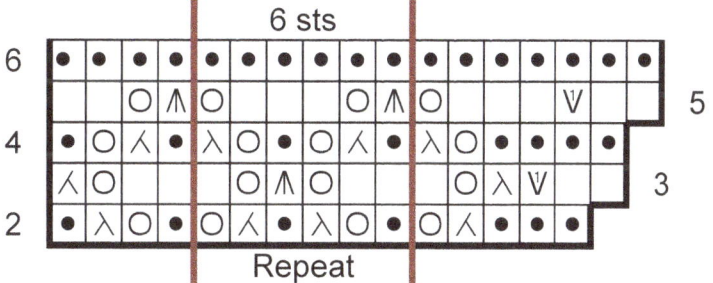

Mystic Cabin – CHART 3

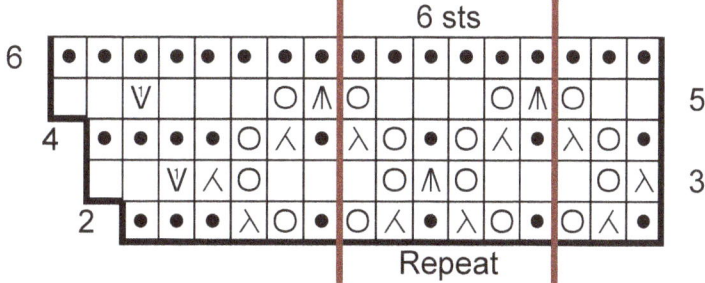

SECTION 3

With first set of needles and [C4 or SC2]:

Row 1 (RS): Pick up and knit 12 sts from side of section 2, k12 from section 1, M1, k2. (27 sts)

Charted Instructions

Follow Chart 3.

Repeat sts in the red box 3 times.

Written Instructions

Row 2 (WS): K3, k2tog, yo, k1, [yo, ssk, k1, k2tog, yo, k1] 3 times, yo, ssk, k1.

Row 3: Ssk, yo, k1, [k2, yo, CDD, yo, k1] 3 times, k2, yo, k2tog, M1, k2.

Row 4: K4, yo, ssk, k1, [k2tog, yo, k1, yo, ssk, k1] 3 times, k2tog, yo, k1.

Row 5: K2, yo, [CDD, yo, k3, yo] 3 times, CDD, yo, k3, M1, k2.

Row 6: Knit.

With [C3 or SC1]:
Row 7: K until 2 sts rem, M1, k2.

Row 8: Knit.

Work rows 7-8 nine times. (38 sts)

SECTION 4

With second set of needles and [C5 or SC2]:

Row 1 (RS): K2 from section 2, M1, k24, then pick up and knit 12 sts from the side of section 3 (one for each purl bump). (39 sts)

Charted Instructions

Follow Chart 2.

Repeat sts in the red box 5 times.

Written Instructions

Row 2 (WS): K1, k2tog, yo, k1, [yo, ssk, k1, k2tog, yo, k1] 5 times, yo, ssk, k3.

Row 3: K2, M1, ssk, yo, k1, [k2, yo, CDD, yo, k1] 5 times, k2, yo, k2tog.

Row 4: K1, yo, ssk, k1, [k2tog, yo, k1, yo, ssk, k1] 5 times, k2tog, yo, k4.

Row 5: K2, M1, k3, yo, [CDD, yo, k3, yo] 5 times, CDD, yo, k2.

Row 6: Knit.

With [C4 or SC1]:
Row 7: K2, M1, k to the end.

Row 8: Knit.

Work rows 7-8 nine times. (50 sts)

SECTION 5

With first set of needles and [C2 or SC2]:

Row 1 (RS): Pick up and knit 12 sts from side of section 4, k36 from section 3, M1, k2. (51 sts)

Charted Instructions

Follow Chart 3.

Repeat sts in the red box 7 times.

Written Instructions

Row 2 (WS): K3, k2tog, yo, k1, [yo, ssk, k1, k2tog, yo, k1] 7 times, yo, ssk, k1.

Row 3: Ssk, yo, k1, [k2, yo, CDD, yo, k1] 7 times, k2, yo, k2tog, M1, k2.

Row 4: K4, yo, ssk, k1, [k2tog, yo, k1, yo, ssk, k1] 7 times, k2tog, yo, k1.

Row 5: K2, yo, [CDD, yo, k3, yo] 7 times, CDD, yo, k3, M1, k2.

Row 6: Knit.

With [C1 or SC1]:
Row 7: K until 2 sts rem, M1, k2.

Row 8: Knit.

Work rows 7-8 nine times. (62 sts)

SECTION 6

With second set of needles and [C3 or SC2]:

Row 1 (RS): K2 from section 4, M1, k48, then pick up and knit 12 sts from the side of section 5 (one for each purl bump). (63 sts)

Charted Instructions

Follow Chart 2.

Repeat sts in the red box 9 times.

Written Instructions

Row 2 (WS): K1, k2tog, yo, k1, [yo, ssk, k1, k2tog, yo, k1] 9 times, yo, ssk, k3.

Row 3: K2, M1, ssk, yo, k1, [k2, yo, CDD, yo, k1] 9 times, k2, yo, k2tog.

Row 4: K1, yo, ssk, k1, [k2tog, yo, k1, yo, ssk, k1] 9 times, k2tog, yo, k4.

Row 5: K2, M1, k3, yo, [CDD, yo, k3, yo] 9 times, CDD, yo, k2.

Row 6: Knit.

With [C2 or SC1]:
Row 7: K2, M1, k to the end.

Row 8: Knit.

Work rows 7-8 nine times. (74 sts)

SECTION 7

With first set of needles and [C4 or SC2]:

Row 1 (RS): Pick up and knit 12 sts from side of section 6, k60 from section 5, M1, k2. (75 sts)

Charted Instructions

Follow Chart 3.

Repeat sts in the red box 11 times.

Written Instructions

Row 2 (WS): K3, k2tog, yo, k1, [yo, ssk, k1, k2tog, yo, k1] 11 times, yo, ssk, k1.

Row 3: Ssk, yo, k1, [k2, yo, CDD, yo, k1] 11 times, k2, yo, k2tog, M1, k2.

Row 4: K4, yo, ssk, k1, [k2tog, yo, k1, yo, ssk, k1] 11 times, k2tog, yo, k1.

Row 5: K2, yo, [CDD, yo, k3, yo] 11 times, CDD, yo, k3, M1, k2.

Row 6: Knit.

With [C3 or SC1]:
Row 7: K until 2 sts rem, M1, k2.

Row 8: Knit.

Work rows 7-8 nine times. (86 sts)

SECTION 8

With second set of needles and [C5 or SC2]:

Row 1 (RS): K2 from section 6, M1, k72, then pick up and knit 12 sts from the side of section 7 (one for each purl bump). (87 sts)

Charted Instructions

Follow Chart 2.

Repeat sts in the red box 13 times.

Written Instructions

Row 2 (WS): K1, k2tog, yo, k1, [yo, ssk, k1, k2tog, yo, k1] 13 times, yo, ssk, k3.

Row 3: K2, M1, ssk, yo, k1, [k2, yo, CDD, yo, k1] 13 times, k2, yo, k2tog.

Row 4: K1, yo, ssk, k1, [k2tog, yo, k1, yo, ssk, k1] 13 times, k2tog, yo, k4.

Row 5: K2, M1, k3, yo, [CDD, yo, k3, yo] 13 times, CDD, yo, k2.

Row 6: Knit.

With [C4 or SC1]:
Row 7: K2, M1, k to the end.

Row 8: Knit.

Work rows 7-8 nine times. (98 sts)

SECTION 9

With first set of needles and [C2 or SC2]:

Row 1 (RS): Pick up and knit 12 sts from side of section 8, k84 from section 7, M1, k2. (99 sts)

Charted Instructions

Follow Chart 3.

Repeat sts in the red box 15 times.

Written Instructions

Row 2 (WS): K3, k2tog, yo, k1, [yo, ssk, k1, k2tog, yo, k1] 15 times, yo, ssk, k1.

Row 3: Ssk, yo, k1, [k2, yo, CDD, yo, k1] 15 times, k2, yo, k2tog, M1, k2.

Row 4: K4, yo, ssk, k1, [k2tog, yo, k1, yo, ssk, k1] 15 times, k2tog, yo, k1.

Row 5: K2, yo, [CDD, yo, k3, yo] 15 times, CDD, yo, k3, M1, k2.

Row 6: Knit.

With [C1 or SC1]:
Row 7: K until 2 sts rem, M1, k2.

Row 8: Knit.

Work rows 7-8 nine times. (110 sts)

SECTION 10

With second set of needles and [C3 or SC2]:

Row 1 (RS): K2 from section 8, M1, k96, then pick up and knit 12 sts from the side of section 9 (one for each purl bump). (111 sts)

Charted Instructions

Follow Chart 2.

Repeat sts in the red box 17 times.

Written Instructions

Row 2 (WS): K1, k2tog, yo, k1, [yo, ssk, k1, k2tog, yo, k1] 17 times, yo, ssk, k3.

Row 3: K2, M1, ssk, yo, k1, [k2, yo, CDD, yo, k1] 17 times, k2, yo, k2tog.

Row 4: K1, yo, ssk, k1, [k2tog, yo, k1, yo, ssk, k1] 17 times, k2tog, yo, k4.

Row 5: K2, M1, k3, yo, [CDD, yo, k3, yo] 17 times, CDD, yo, k2.

Row 6: Knit.

With [C2 or SC1]:
Row 7: K2, M1, k to the end.

Row 8: Knit.

Work rows 7-8 nine times. (122 sts)

SECTION 11

With first set of needles and [C4 or SC2]:

Row 1 (RS): Pick up and knit 12 sts from side of section 10, k108 from section 9, M1, k2. (123 sts)

Charted Instructions

Follow Chart 3.

Repeat sts in the red box 19 times.

Written Instructions

Row 2 (WS): K3, k2tog, yo, k1, [yo, ssk, k1, k2tog, yo, k1] 19 times, yo, ssk, k1.

Row 3: Ssk, yo, k1, [k2, yo, CDD, yo, k1] 19 times, k2, yo, k2tog, M1, k2.

Row 4: K4, yo, ssk, k1, [k2tog, yo, k1, yo, ssk, k1] 19 times, k2tog, yo, k1.

Row 5: K2, yo, [CDD, yo, k3, yo] 19 times, CDD, yo, k3, M1, k2.

Row 6: Knit.

With [C3 or SC1]:
Row 7: K until 2 sts rem, M1, k2.

Row 8: Knit.

Work rows 7-8 nine times. (134 sts)

OPTIONAL

If you would like to enlarge your shawl, keep working alternating EVEN and ODD sections (making sure that you end with an ODD section).

NOTE: This will require more yarn than 1 gradient kit of Pebble Sock from Black Trillium Yarn.

EVEN SECTIONS

With second set of needles and [C5/C3 or SC2]:

Row 1 (RS): K2 from previous even section, M1, k all remaining sts, then pick up and knit 12 sts from the side of previous odd section (one for each purl bump).

[stitch count = stitch count at the end of previous odd section + 1]

Charted Instructions

Follow Chart 2.

Repeat sts in the red box 2 more times than in the previous even section (X times).

Written Instructions

Row 2 (WS): K1, k2tog, yo, k1, [yo, ssk, k1, k2tog, yo, k1] X times, yo, ssk, k3.

Row 3: K2, M1, ssk, yo, k1, [k2, yo, CDD, yo, k1] X times, k2, yo, k2tog.

Row 4: K1, yo, ssk, k1, [k2tog, yo, k1, yo, ssk, k1] X times, k2tog, yo, k4.

Row 5: K2, M1, k3, yo, [CDD, yo, k3, yo] 9 times, CDD, yo, k2.

Row 6: Knit.

With [C2 or SC1]:
With [C4/C2 or SC1]:
Row 7: K2, M1, k to the end.

Row 8: Knit.

Work rows 7-8 nine times.

[stitch count = stitch count at the end of row 1 + 11]

ODD SECTIONS

With first set of needles and [C2/C4 or SC2]:

Row 1 (RS): Pick up and knit 12 sts from side of section 10, k until 2 sts remain from section 9, M1, k2.

[stitch count = stitch count at the end of previous even section + 1]

Charted Instructions

Follow Chart 3.

Repeat sts in the red box 2 more times than in the previous even section (X times).

Written Instructions

Row 2 (WS): K3, k2tog, yo, k1, [yo, ssk, k1, k2tog, yo, k1] X times, yo, ssk, k1.

Row 3: Ssk, yo, k1, [k2, yo, CDD, yo, k1] X times, k2, yo, k2tog, M1, k2.

Row 4: K4, yo, ssk, k1, [k2tog, yo, k1, yo, ssk, k1] X times, k2tog, yo, k1.

Row 5: K2, yo, [CDD, yo, k3, yo] 19 times, CDD, yo, k3, M1, k2.

Row 6: Knit.

With [C1/C3 or SC1]:
Row 7: K until 2 sts rem, M1, k2.

Row 8: Knit.

Work rows 7-8 nine times.

[stitch count = stitch count at the end of row 1 + 11]

EDGING

With second set of needles and [C1 or SC2]:

Row 1 (RS): K2 from section 10, M1, k120, pickup and knit 12 sts from side of section 11, PM, M1, k132 from section 11, M1, k2. [271 sts]

NOTE: If you have worked more than 11 sections above, row 1 becomes: K2 from last even section, M1, k rem sts from last even section, pickup and knit 12 sts from side of last odd section, PM, M1, k from last odd section until 2 sts rem, M1, k2.

[stitch-count = 2 * stitch count at the end of previous odd section + 3]

Charted Instructions

Follow Mystic Cabin EDGING chart 1.

Work rows 2-6 with [C1 or SC2].

Work rows 7-8 with [C2 or SC2]. (283 sts)

Follow Mystic Cabin EDGING chart 1.

Work rows 9-10 with [C2 or SC2].

Work rows 11-12 with [C3 or SC2].

Work rows 13-18 with [C4 or SC2].

Work rows 19-26 with [C5 or SC2]. (323 sts)

Written Instructions

Row 2 (WS): K3, k2tog, yo, [k1, yo, ssk, k1, k2tog, yo] 21 times, k1, yo, ssk, k3, k2tog, yo, k1, [yo, ssk, k1, k2tog, yo, k1] 21 times, yo, ssk, k3.

Row 3: K2, M1, Ssk, yo, k1, [k2, yo, CDD, yo, k1] 21 times, k2, yo, k2tog, yo, k1, yo, ssk, yo, k2, [k1, yo, CDD, yo, k2] 21 times, k1, yo, k2tog, M1, k2.

Row 4: K4, yo, ssk, [k1, k2tog, yo, k1, yo, ssk] 21 times, k1, k2tog, yo, k5, yo, ssk, k1, [k2tog, yo, k1, yo, ssk, k1] 21 times, k2tog, yo, k4.

Row 5: K2, M1, k3, yo, [CDD, yo, k3, yo] 21 times, CDD, yo, k3, yo, k1, yo, k3, yo, CDD, [yo, k3, yo, CDD] 21 times, yo, k3, M1, k2.

Row 6: Knit.

With [C2 or SC2]:

Row 7: K2, M1, k5, [k6] 21 times, k6, yo, k1, yo, k6, [k6] 21 times, k5, M1, k2.

Row 8: Knit. [283 sts]

With [C2 or SC2]:

Row 9 (RS): K2, M1, ssk, k4, yo, [k1, yo, k4, CDD, k4, yo] 11 times, [k1, yo] 2 times, [k1, yo, k4, CDD, k4, yo] 11 times, k1, yo, k4, k2tog, M1, k2.

Row 10: Knit.

With [C3 or SC2]:

Row 11: K2, M1, k1, ssk, k4, yo, [k1, yo, k4, CDD, k4, yo] 11 times, [k1, yo, k1, yo] 2 times, [k1, yo, k4, CDD, k4, yo] 11 times, k1, yo, k4, k2tog, k1, M1, k2.

Row 12: Knit.

With [C4 or SC2]:

Row 13: K2, M1, k2, ssk, k4, yo, [k1, yo, k4, CDD, k4, yo] 11 times, [k1, yo, k3, yo] 2 times, [k1, yo, k4, CDD, k4, yo] 11 times, k1, yo, k4, k2tog, k2, M1, k2.

Row 14: Knit.

Row 15: K2, M1, k3, ssk, k4, yo, [k1, yo, k4, CDD, k4, yo] 11 times, [k1, yo, k5, yo] 2 times, [k1, yo, k4, CDD, k4, yo] 11 times, k1, yo, k4, k2tog, k3, M1, k2.

Row 16: Knit.

Row 17: K2, M1, k4, ssk, k4, yo, [k1, yo, k4, CDD, k4, yo] 11 times, [k1, yo, k7, yo] 2 times, [k1, yo, k4, CDD, k4, yo] 11 times, k1, yo, k4, k2tog, k4, M1, k2.

Row 18: Knit.

With [C5 or SC2]:

Row 19: K2, M1, k5, ssk, k4, yo, [k1, yo, k4, CDD, k4, yo] 11 times, [k1, yo, k9, yo] 2 times, [k1, yo, k4, CDD, k4, yo] 11 times, k1, yo, k4, k2tog, k5, M1, k2.

Row 20: Knit.

Row 21: K2, M1, k1, yo, k4, CDD, k4, yo [k1, yo, k4, CDD, k4, yo] 11 times, [k1, yo, k4, CDD, k4, yo] 2 times, [k1, yo, k4, CDD, k4, yo] 11 times, k1, yo, k4, CDD, k4, yo, k1, M1, k2.

Row 22: Knit.

Row 23: K2, M1, k2, yo, k4, CDD, k4, yo [k1, yo, k4, CDD, k4, yo] 11 times, [k1, yo, k4, CDD, k4, yo] 2 times, [k1, yo, k4, CDD, k4, yo] 11 times, k1, yo, k4, CDD, k4, yo, k2, M1, k2.

Row 24: Knit.

Mystic Cabin – EDGING 1   Mystic Cabin – EDGING 2

Row 25: K2, M1, k3, yo, k4, CDD, k4, yo [k1, yo, k4, CDD, k4, yo] 11 times, [k1, yo, k4, CDD, k4, yo] 2 times, [k1, yo, k4, CDD, k4, yo] 11 times, k1, yo, k4, CDD, k4, yo, k3, M1, k2.

Row 26: Knit. (323 sts)

Then bind off as follows:
K2, *return to left needle, k2tog through back loop, k1, repeat from * until no unworked stitches remain.

FINISHING INSTRUCTIONS

Sew in ends and block.

When blocking, pull out the knit stitch between the yarn overs to points.

mystic junction

You think you know where you're going, when life throws you a curveball. When you thought you were heading straight, you take a sharp turn to the right. Mystic Junction is a rectangular stole with an unusual construction.

Mystic Junction

MATERIALS

1 skein each of Chameleon Sock from indigodragonfly (63% extra fine superwash merino, 20% cashmere, 17% silk, 400 yds/400 g) in *Sage Fright* and *Sargasm*

3.75 mm [US 6] needles

Stitch markers

Large-eyed, blunt needle

GAUGE

12 sts and 24 rows = 4 in [10 cm] in pattern, blocked

FINISHED (BLOCKED) SIZE

length: 180 (201) cm [71 (79) in], adjustable in pattern

width: 50 cm (20 in)

INSTRUCTIONS

[C1] CO 3 sts.

Set-up Row 1-280 (328): K3.

Pick-up Row: K3, pick-up and knit 140 (164) sts (1 st for each purl-bump). [143 (167) sts]

Note: If you would like to further adjust the length of the stole, knit (a multiple of) 16 extra 3-stitch-rows, and pick up (a multiple of) 8 extra stitches in the pick-up row.

Last Set-up Row: K all sts.

Section 1

With [C1], work rows 1-32. Work the repeat 16 (19) times.

See Chart A

Section 2

With [C2], work rows 33-48. Work the first repeat 1 time, and the second repeat 18 (21) times.

Then work rows 33-48 again. Work the first repeat 2 times, and the second repeat 19 (22) times.

See Chart B

Section 3

With [C1], work rows 65-80. Work the first repeat 3 times, and the second repeat 20 (23) times.

See Chart C

Section 4

With [C2], work rows 81-96. Work the first repeat 4 times, and the second repeat 21 (24) times.

See Chart D

Section 5

With [C1], work rows 97-104. Work the first repeat 5 times, and the second repeat 22 (25) times.

See Chart E

Section 6

With [C2], work rows 97-104. Work the first repeat 6 times, and the second repeat 23 (26) times.

See Chart F

Section 7

With [C1], work rows 113-114.

With [C2], work rows 115-116.

With [C1], work rows 117-118.

With [C2], work rows 119-120.

Work the first repeat 6 times, and the second repeat 23 (26) times.

See Chart G

With [C1]:
Rows 121-124: K all sts.

FINISHING INSTRUCTIONS

Bind off as follows: K1, [p1, return to left needle, k2tog through back loop, k1, return to left needle, k2tog through back loop] repeat until no stitches remain.

Sew in ends and block.

Mystic Junction – CHART A

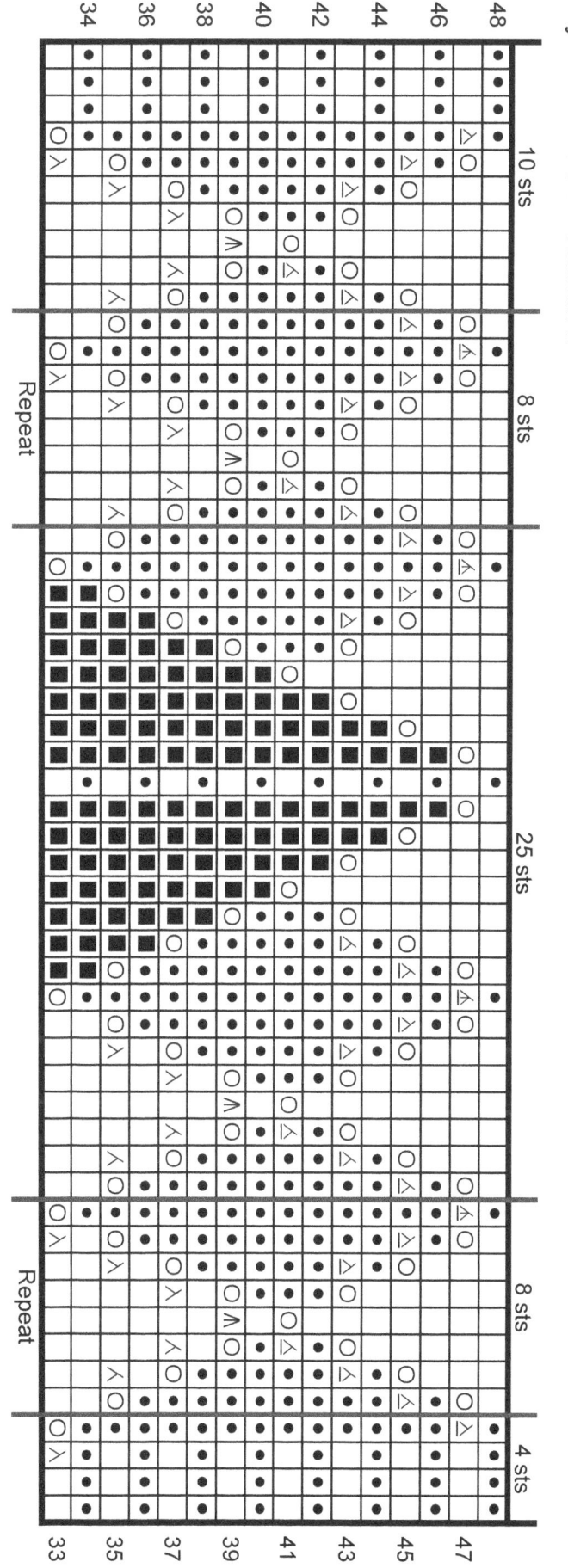

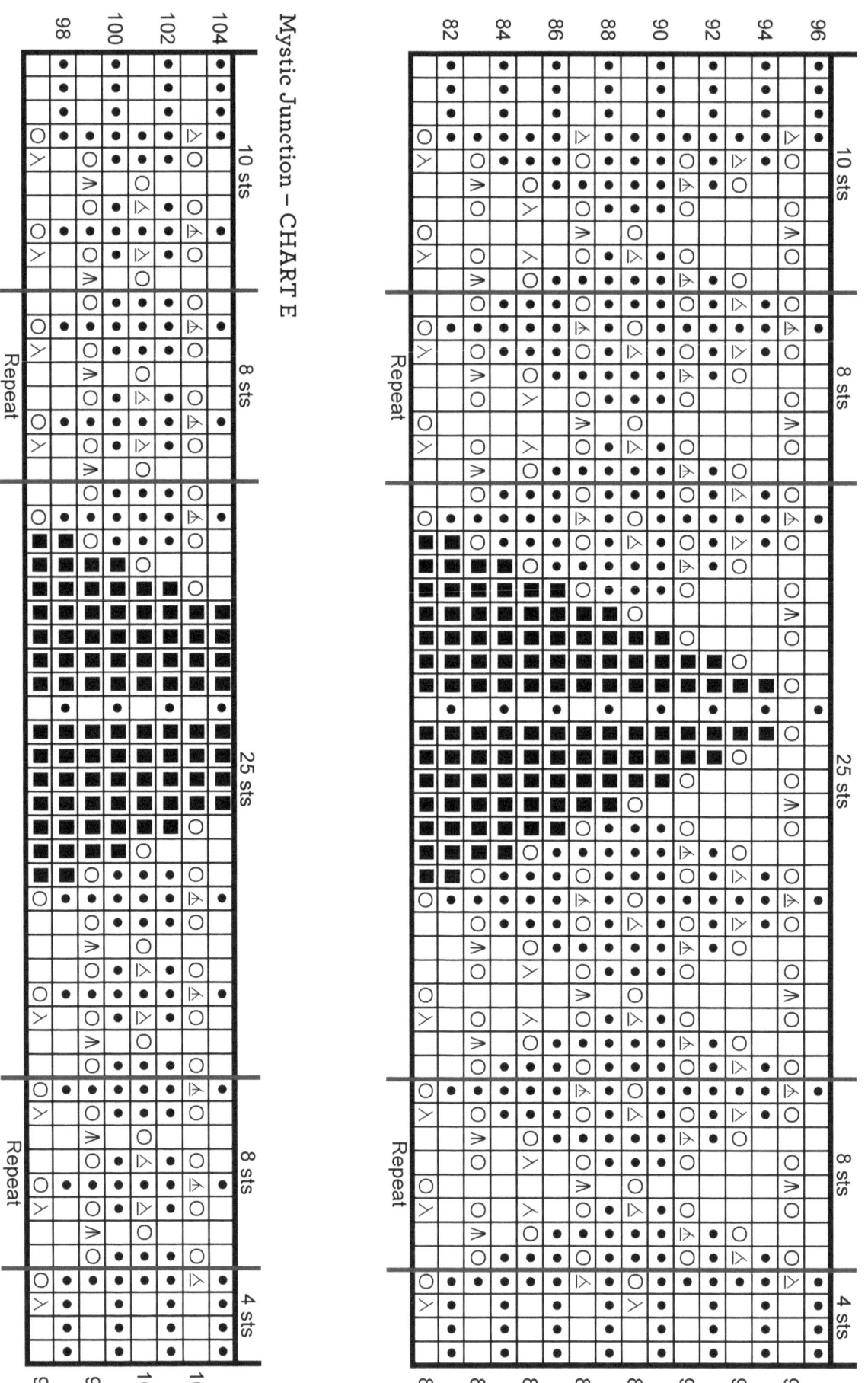

mystic sea witch

Sea Witches are witches who can help or hinder sailors out on the stormy sea. They draw power from the moon, tides, and the weather, and were believed to have complete control over the seas. They even have the power to control the fates of ships and seamen.

They can control the wind by using a rope tied into three knots. When the three knots are tied in the proper magical way, the wind is bound up in them. Witches gave, or sometimes sold, these magic knots to sailors to help them experience safe voyages.

The release of one knot brought a gentle, south-westerly wind; two knots, a strong north wind; and three knots, a tempest.

Mystic Sea Witch

MATERIALS

1 gradient kit of Fairy Sock fine from Yarn Fairy (100% merino, 1792 m/ 400 g, 4 shades of one color) or similar yarn

4.5 mm [US 7] needles

4.5 mm [US 7] crochet hook (optional)

Stitch markers

Large-eyed, blunt needle

GAUGE

20 sts and 24 rows = 4 in [10 cm] in stockinette stitch, blocked

FINISHED (BLOCKED) SIZE

Diameter: 180 cm [71 in]

CIRCULAR SHAWL INSTRUCTIONS

CO 9 sts using invisible loop.

Divide evenly on 3 DPNs (switch to circular needles when you have enough stitches on the needles, or use magic loop).

Rnd 1: K9, place a marker to mark the beginning of the rnds.

Rnd 2: [K1, yo] repeat 9 times. (18 sts)

Rnd 3-5: Knit.

Rnd 6: [K1, yo] repeat 18 times. (36 sts)

Rnd 7-12: Knit.

Rnd 13: [K1,yo] repeat 36 times. (72 sts)

Section 1

Work Chart A 12 times around.

All even rnds in Section 1 are knit.

Rnd 27: [K1, yo] repeat 72 times. (144 sts)

Rnd 28: Knit.

Section 2

Work Chart B 12 times around.

All even rnds in Section 2 are knit.

Rnd 53: [K1, yo] repeat 144 times. (288 sts)

Rnd 54: Knit.

Section 3

Work Chart C 12 times around.

In this section, the start of Rnd will be shifted during rnd 92.

Even rnds are worked as follows:

Rnds 56-90: K288.

Rnd 92: K288, RM, k6, PM.

Rnds 94-102: K288.

Rnd 103: [K1, yo] repeat 288 times. (576 sts)

Rnd 104: K576, RM, k12, PM.

Section 4

Work Chart D 12 times around.

All even rnds in Section 4 are knit.

Rnd 199: P575 stitches (stop one stitch short of completing the round), then bind off as follows with a crochet hook:

crochet 3 stitches together, *work 9 stitches of crochet chain, crochet the next 3 stitches from the edge, repeat from * until no unworked stitches remain, work 9 stitches of crochet chain, attach to beginning of round.

Sew in ends and block. When blocking, pull each of the 24 peaks of the pattern to a point for the edging.

Mystic Sea Witch – CHART A

Mystic Sea Witch – CHART B

Mystic Sea Witch – CHART C

Mystic Sea Witch – CHART D

SEMI-CIRCULAR SHAWL INSTRUCTIONS

CO 2 sts by knitting them on.

Setup row 1: Kfb, kfb. (4 sts)

Setup row 2: Kfb 4 times. (8 sts)

Setup row 3: K2, p4, k2.

All WS rows (even rows) are K2, p until 2 sts remain, k2.

Row 1: K2, [yo, k1] repeat 4 times, yo, k2. (13 sts)

Row 3: K13.

Row 5: K2, [k1, yo] repeat 9 times, k2. (22 sts)

Row 7: K22.

Row 9-12: as rows 7-8.

Row 13: K2, [k1,yo] repeat 18 times, k2. (40 sts)

Note: all even rows from this point are K2, p to the last 2 stitches, k2.

Section 1

RS rows: [Charted Row]

Row 27: K2, [k1, yo] repeat 36 times, k2. (76 sts)

Row 28: K2, p72, k2.

Section 2

Chart B semi.

RS rows: [Charted Row]

Row 53: K2, [k1, yo] repeat 72 times, k2. (148 sts)

Row 54: K2, p144, k2.

Section 3

Chart C semi.

RS rows: [Charted Row]

Row 103: K2, [k1, yo] repeat 144 times, k2. (292 sts)

Row 104: K2, p288, k2.

Section 4

Chart D semi.

RS rows: [Charted Row]

Bind off as follows with a crochet hook:

crochet 4 stitches together, *work 9 stitches of crochet chain, crochet the next 3 stitches from the edge, repeat from * until no unworked stitches remain.

Sew in ends and block. When blocking, pull each of the 13 peaks of the pattern to a point for the edging.

Mystic Sea Witch Semi-Circular – CHART A

Mystic Sea Witch Semi-Circular – CHART B

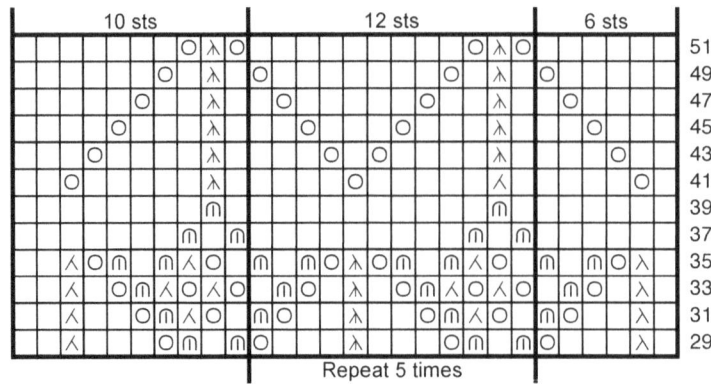

Mystic Sea Witch Semi-Circular – CHART C

Mystic Sea Witch Semi-Circular – CHART D

mystic haven

Mystic Haven is a small shawl that breaks up and works a gradient from both ends of the skein. It's a nice, relaxing knit that lets the yarn shine.

Mystic Haven

MATERIALS

1 skein of Greatest of Ease from KnitCircus Yarns (80% merino, 20% nylon, 400 yds/100 g) or similar yarn

4.5 mm [US 7] needles

Stitch markers

Large-eyed, blunt needle

FINISHED (BLOCKED) SIZE

Wingspan: 152 cm (60 in), height: 50 cm (19.5 in)

If you are knitting the shawl with a gradient, make sure you have access to both ends of the gradient. The white rows are worked with one end of the gradient, and the shaded gray rows with the other end. The colors will change over time, and by the time you reach the end of the shawl, you will be somewhere in the middle of the gradient.

If you are knitting the shawl with two different solid colors, work the white rows in color 1 and the shaded gray rows with color 2, unless otherwise noted.

INSTRUCTIONS

CO 4 sts. Start working the charts. All rows are charted.

Edging

Do not break the yarn.

At this point, you have 106 sts.

CO 4 sts.

Work rows 1-13 of the edging chart, then work rows 6-13 TWENTY-FOUR more times, and then work rows 206-212. BO 9 sts.

Sew in ends and block.

Mystic Haven – EDGING

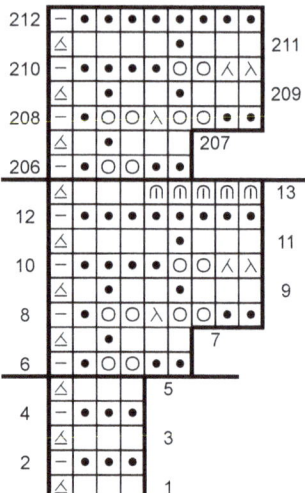

Mystic Haven – CHART A

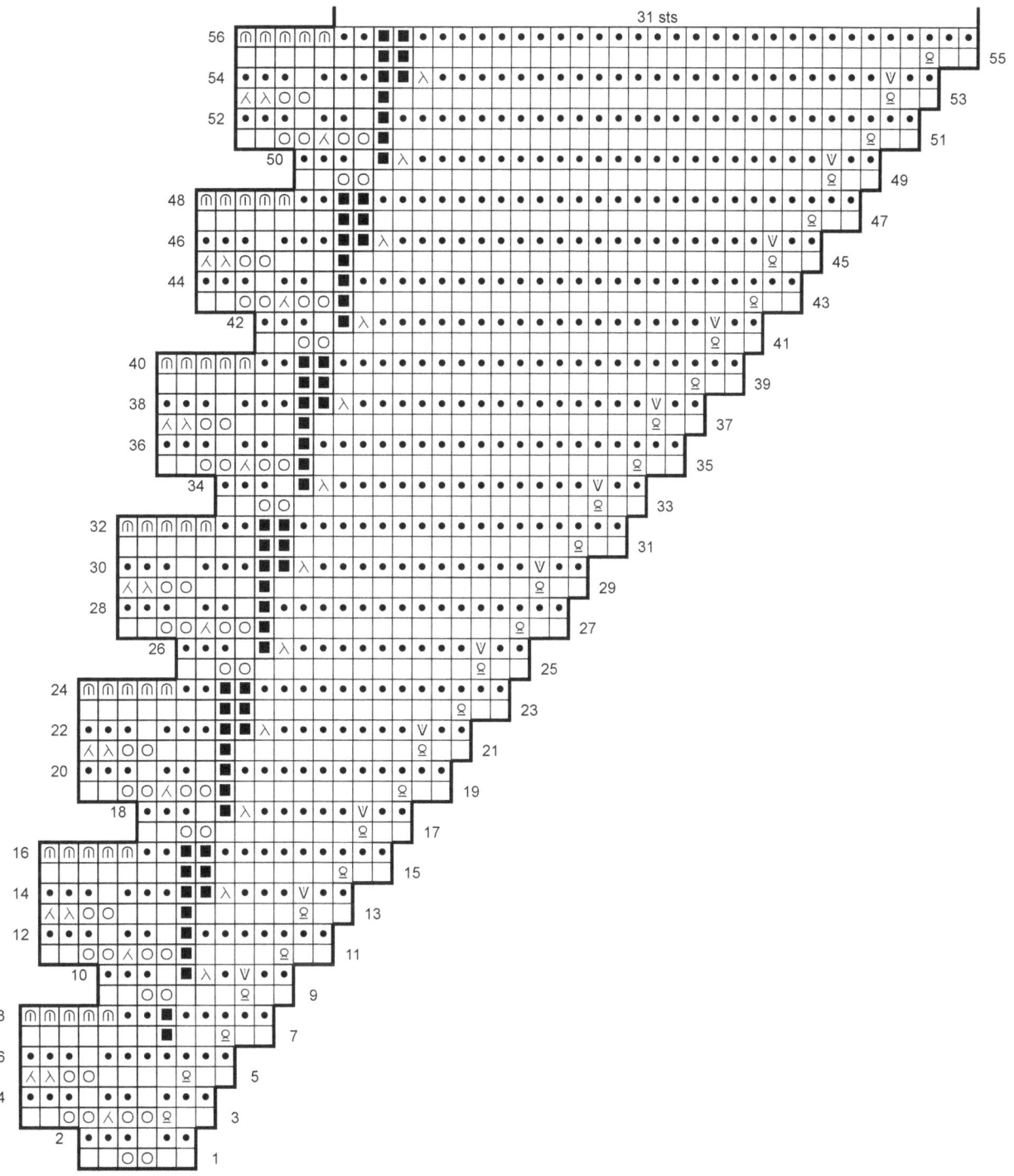

Mystic Haven – CHART B

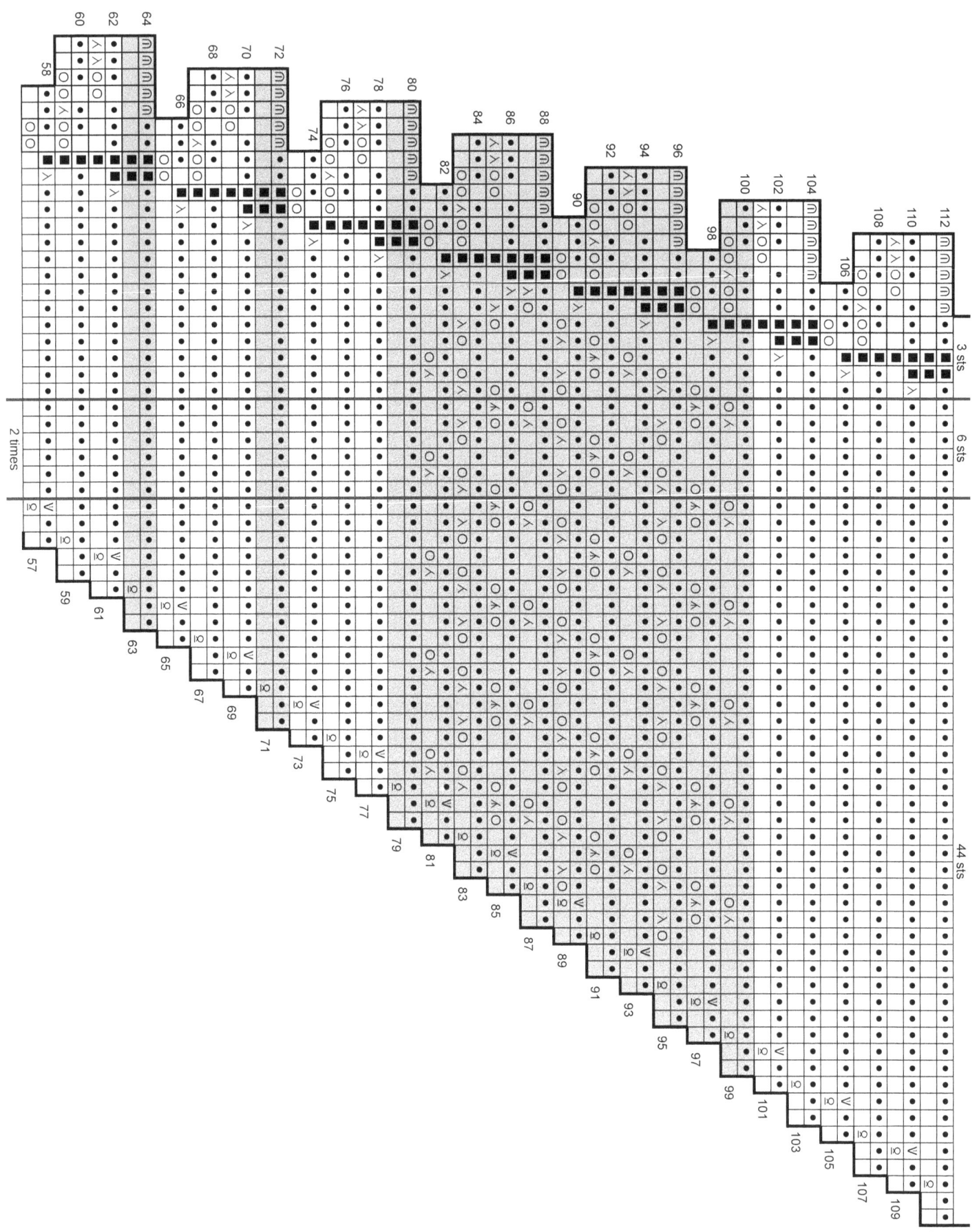

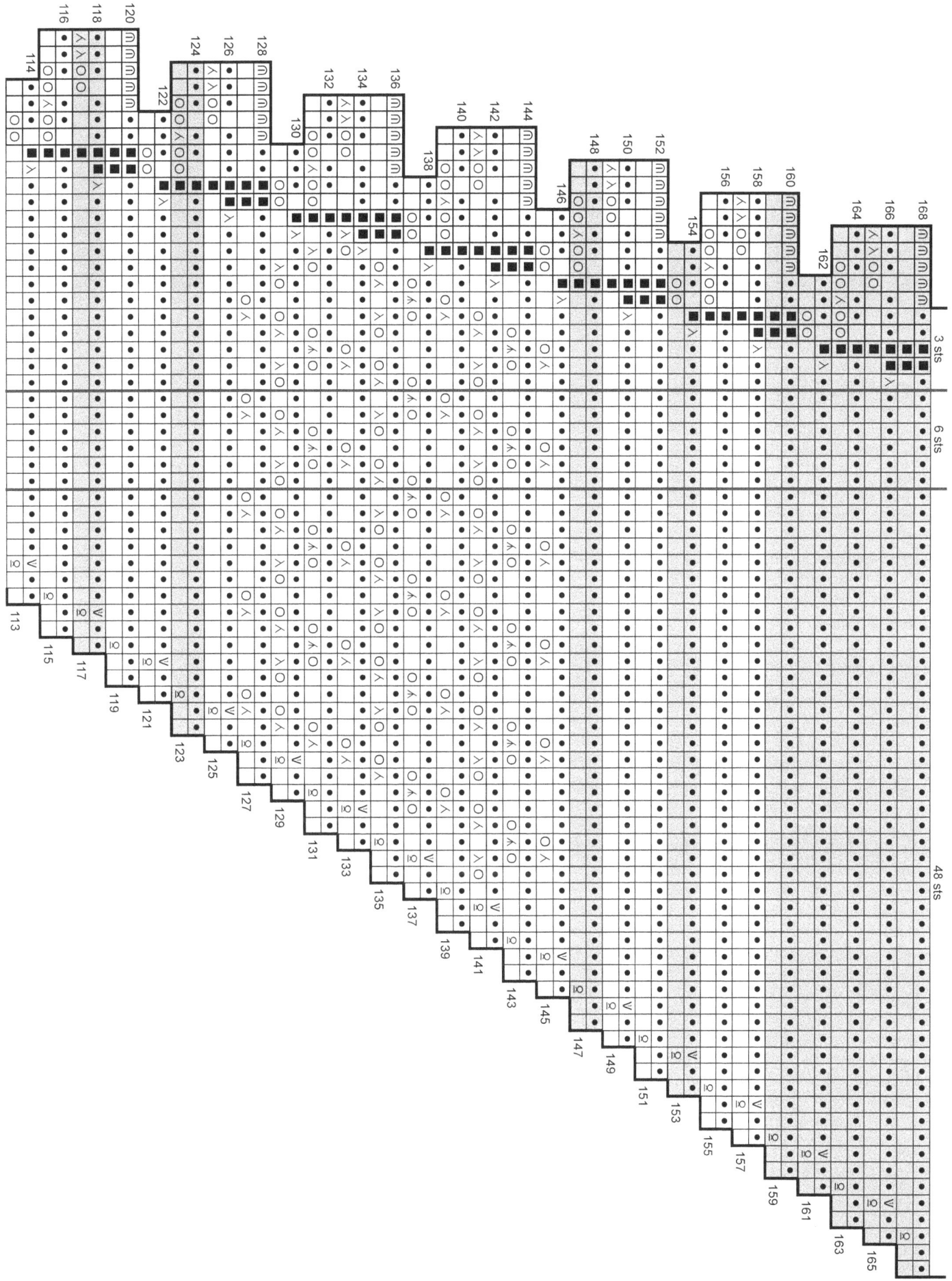

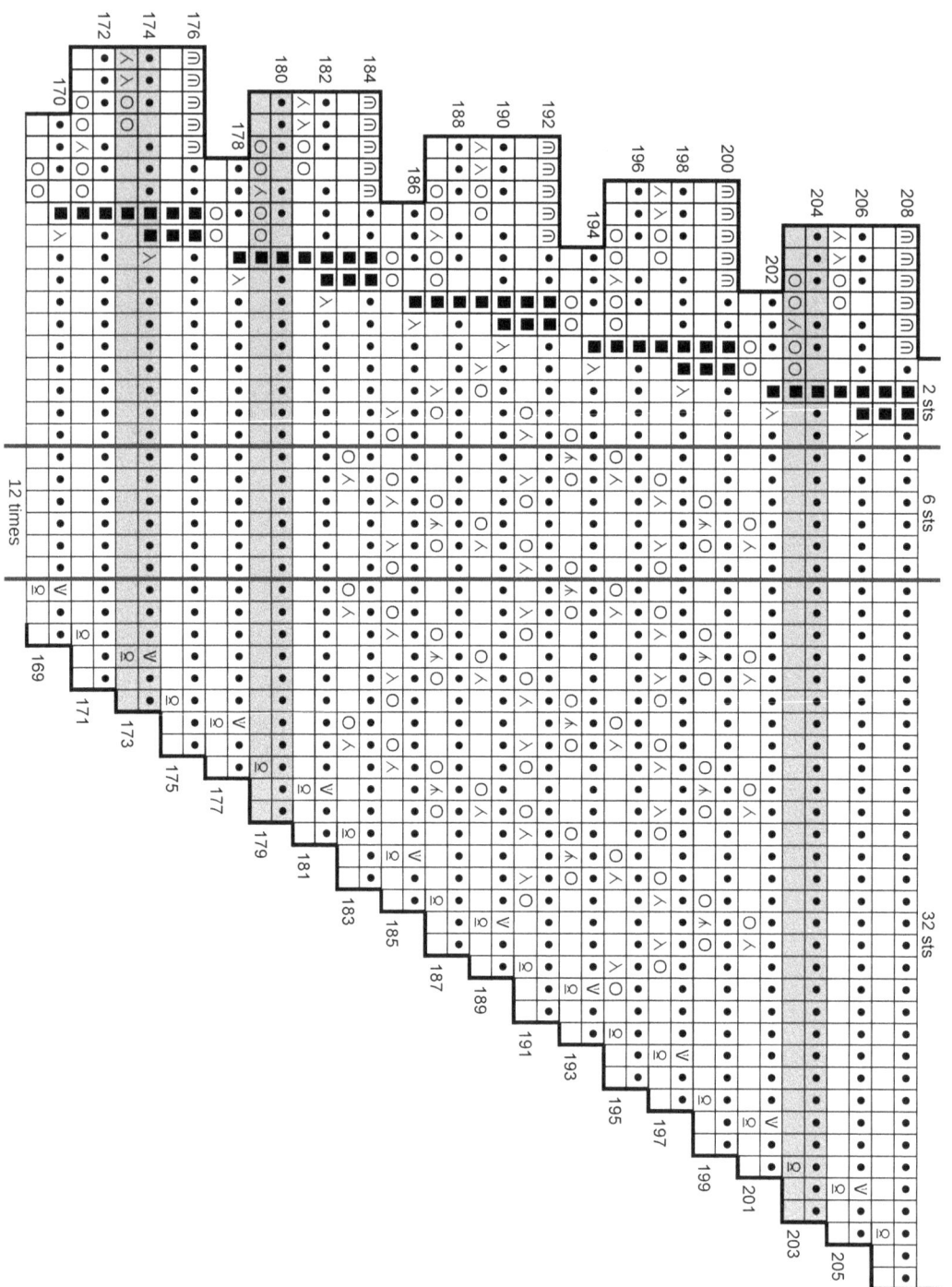

mystic sunset

The golden yellow sun grows heavy after a long day and sinks lower and lower. It lingers on the horizon and then dips below, leaving the sky a brilliant cascade of colors - orange to red, fading to pink and into a deep purple night sky. Mystic Sunset pairs a tangerine to ultraviolet gradient set with a solid color to create a spectacular sunset shawl in which to wrap yourself.

Mystic Sunset

MATERIALS

1 skein Fiber Optics Yarn Foot Notes [80% superwash merino wool, 20% nylon; 420 yds/381 m per 114 g] in *Sterling* [C1]

1 box Fiber Optics Yarn Foot Notes Paintbox Gradient [80% superwash merino wool, 20% nylon; 450 yds/411 m per 122 g] in *Tangerine-Ultraviolet* [C2]

US 7 [4.5 mm] needles

Large-eyed, blunt needle

Stitch markers

GAUGE

15 sts and 28 rows = 4 in [10 cm] in garter stitch, blocked

FINISHED (BLOCKED) SIZE

Wingspan: 80 in [202 cm]
Height: 24 in [61 cm]

INSTRUCTIONS

With C1:
CO 2 sts using a provisional cast on.

Set-up Row 1-10: K2.

Set-up Row 11: K2, pick up and knit 1 st in each purl bump of the garter tab, pick up and knit 2 sts from the provisional cast on. (9 sts)

Set-up Row 12: Knit.

Set-up Row 13: K2, [yo, k1] 6 times, k1. (15 sts)

Set-up Row 14: Knit.

[C1] Row 1: K2, [yo, k1] 3 times, knit until 4 sts rem, [yo, k1] 3 times, k1.

Row 2: Knit.

Row 3-12: As rows 1-2.

With C2:
Row 13: Sl5, [ky5, slwyib] 7 times, turn work.

Row 14: Sl1, [aster, slwyif] 7 times, sl4 with yarn in front.

With C1:
Row 15: K2, [yo, k1] 3 times, k5, [sl1 knitwise, pick up C2 bar, replace 2 sts on left needle and k both stitches together through the back loop, k5] 6 times, [k1, yo] 3 times, k2.

Row 16: Knit.

With C2:
Row 17: Sl5, [ky5, slwyib] 8 times, turn work.

Row 18: Sl1, [aster, slwyif] 8 times, sl4 with yarn in front.

With C1:
Row 19: K2, [yo, k1] 3 times, k5, [sl1 knitwise, pick up C2 bar, replace 2 sts on left needle and k both stitches together through the back loop, k5] 7 times, [k1, yo] 3 times, k2.

Row 20: Knit.

With C1:
Row 21: K2, [yo, k1] 3 times, knit until 4 sts rem, [yo, k1] 3 times, k1.

Row 22: Knit.

Row 23-32: As rows 21-22.

With C2:
Row 33: Sl5, [ky5, slwyib] repeat until 4 sts rem, turn work.

Row 34: Sl1, [aster, slwyif] repeat until 4 sts rem, sl4 with yarn in front.

With C1:
Row 35: K2, [yo, k1] 3 times, k5, [sl1 knitwise, pick up C2 bar, replace 2 sts on left needle and k both stitches together through the back loop, k5] repeat until 5 sts rem, [k1, yo] 3 times, k2.

Row 36: Knit.

With C2:
Row 37: Sl5, [ky5, slwyib] repeat until 4 sts rem, turn work.

Row 38: Sl1, [aster, slwyif] 16 times, sl4 with yarn in front.

With C1:
Row 39: K2, [yo, k1] 3 times, k5, [sl1 knitwise, pick up C2 bar, replace 2 sts on left needle and k both stitches together through the back loop, k5] repeat until 5 sts rem, [k1, yo] 3 times, k2.

Row 40: Knit.

Work rows 21-40 THREE more times. (255 sts)

With C2:
Row 101: K2, [yo, k1] 3 times, knit until 4 sts rem, [yo, k1] 3 times, k1.

Row 102: Knit.

With C1:
Row 103-104: As rows 101-102.

With C2:
Row 105-106: As rows 101-102.

With C1:
Row 106-108: As rows 101-102.

With C2:
Row 107-110: As rows 101-102.

With C1:
Row 108-112: As rows 101-102.

With C2:
Row 113: Sl5, [ky5, slwyib] repeat until 4 sts rem, turn work.

Row 114: Sl1, [aster, slwyif] repeat until 4 sts rem, sl4 with yarn in front.

With C1:
Row 115: K2, [yo, k1] 3 times, k5, [sl1 knitwise, pick up C2 bar, replace 2 sts on left needle and k both stitches together through the back loop, k5] repeat until 5 sts rem, [k1, yo] 3 times, k2.

Row 116: Knit.

With C2:
Row 117: Sl5, [ky5, slwyib] repeat until 4 sts rem, turn work.

Row 118: Sl1, [aster, slwyif] 16 times, sl4 with yarn in front.

With C1:
Row 119: K2, [yo, k1] 3 times, k5, [sl1 knitwise, pick up C2 bar, replace 2 sts on left needle and k both stitches together through the back loop, k5] repeat until 5 sts rem, [k1, yo] 3 times, k2.

Row 120: Knit.

Work rows 101-120 ONE more time. [351 sts]

With C2:
Row 141: K2, [yo, k1] 3 times, knit until 4 sts rem, [yo, k1] 3 times, k1.

Row 142: Knit. (357 sts)

FINISHING INSTRUCTIONS

Bind off as follows:

K2, return sts to left needle, k2tog through back loop, [return st to left needle, CO2, k1, (k1, return sts to left needle, k2tog through back loop, k1) 8 times] until 1 unworked st remains, return st to left needle, CO2, k1, (k1, return sts to left needle, k2tog through back loop, k1) until no unworked sts remain.

mystic mist

Mystic Mist was inspired by a crisp fall morning in Rhinebeck, NY. I was driving across the Rhinecliff Bridge to get to the New York Sheep & Wool Festival as the mist rose over the Hudson River. After a while the sun broke through the mist, and I could see the spectacular golds and browns of the fall colors, and I knew I had to knit a tribute. At the festival, I found the perfect yarn to capture the feeling.

For the circular shawl you will need approx. 1300 yards of ngering weight yarn (2 paintboxes +1 matching skein). There is also a semicircular version of the shawl, which uses approx. 650 yards (1 paintbox + 0.5 matching skeins). The shawl is designed for the paintbox gradient kits from Fiber Optic Yarns with a matching solid skein (see below for details), but can also be knit in one solid color, or full gradient.

Mystic Mist

MATERIALS

2 Paintbox Gradient Foot Notes Yarn from Fiber Optic Yarns (80% super wash merino, 20% Nylon 450 yds/122 g, 15 mini-skeins [30 yds each]) in *Steampunk* or similar yarn. 1 skein Foot Notes Yarn from Fiber Optic Yarns (80% super wash merino, 20% Nylon 420 yds/114 g) in *Sterling* or similar yarn

4.5 mm [US 7] circular needles

4.5 mm [US 7] double-pointed needles (optional)

4.5 mm [US 7] crochet hook (optional)

Stitch markers

Large-eyed, blunt needle

GAUGE

13 sts and 20 rows = 4 in [10 cm] in stockinette stitch, blocked

FINISHED (BLOCKED) SIZE

Diameter: 140 cm [55 in]

CIRCULAR SHAWL INSTRUCTIONS

CO 9 sts using invisible loop.

Divide evenly on 3 DPNs (switch to circular needles when you have enough stitches on the needles, or use magic loop).

Rnd 1: K9, place a marker to mark the beginning of the rnds.

Rnd 2: [K1, yo] repeat 9 times. (18 sts)

Rnd 3-5: Knit.

Rnd 6: [K1, yo] repeat 18 times. (36 sts)

Rnd 7-12: Knit Rnd 13: [K1,yo] repeat 36 times. (72 sts)

SECTION 1

Work Chart A 12 times around.

All even rnds in Section 1 are knit.

Rnd 27: [K1, yo] repeat 72 times. (144 sts)

Rnd 28: Knit.

SECTION 2

Work Chart B 12 times around.

All even rnds in Section 2 are knit.

Rnd 53: [K1, yo] repeat 144 times. (288 sts)

Rnd 54: Knit.

SECTION 3

Work Chart C 12 times around.

All even rnds in Section 3 are knit.

Rnd 103: [K1, yo] repeat 288 times. (576 sts)

Rnd 104: K576. No shifting beg of rnd by 12 sts.

SECTION 4

Work Chart D 12 times around.

All even rnds in Section 4 are knit.

Rnd 151: P576.

Rnd 152: K576.

Rnd 153: P575 stitches (stop one stitch short of completing the round), then bind off as follows with a crochet hook: crochet 3 stitches together, *work 9 stitches of crochet chain, crochet the next 3 stitches from the edge, repeat from * until no unworked stitches remain, work 9 stitches of crochet chain, attach to beginning of round. Sew in ends and block. When blocking, pull each of the 24 peaks of the pattern to a point for the edging.

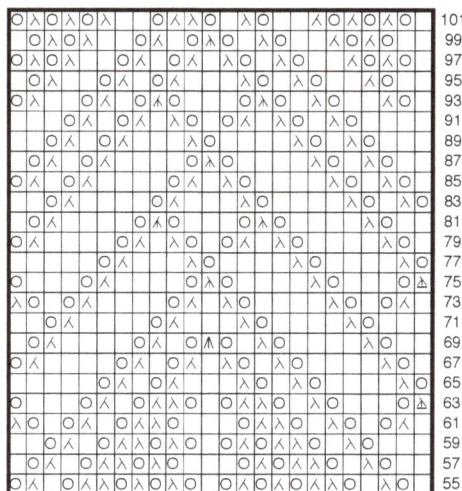

SEMI-CIRCULAR SHAWL INSTRUCTIONS

CO 2 sts by knitting them on.

Setup row 1: Kfb, kfb. (4 sts)

Setup row 2: Kfb 4 times. (8 sts)

Setup row 3: K2, p4, k2.

All WS rows (even rows) are K2, p until 2 sts remain, k2.

Row 1: K2, [yo, k1] repeat 4 times, yo, k2. (13 sts)

Row 3: K13.

Row 5: K2, [k1, yo] repeat 9 times, k2. (22 sts)

Row 7: K22.

Row 9-12: as rows 7-8.

Row 13: K2, [k1,yo] repeat 18 times, k2. (40 sts)

Note: all even rows from this point are K2, p to the last 2 stitches, k2.

SECTION 1

Work Chart A.

RS rows: [Charted Row]

Row 27: k2, [k1, yo] repeat 36 times, k2. (76 sts)

Row 28: k2, p72, k2.

SECTION 2

Work Chart B.

RS rows: [Charted Row]

Row 53: K2, [k1, yo] repeat 72 times, k2. (148 sts)

Row 54: K2, p144, k2.

SECTION 3

Work Chart C.

RS rows: [Charted Row]

Row 103: K2, [k1, yo] repeat 144 times, k2. (292 sts)

Row 104: K2, p288, k2.

SECTION 4

Work Chart D.

RS rows: [Charted Row]

Rnd 151-153: Knit.

Bind off as follows with a crochet hook: crochet 4 stitches together, *work 9 stitches of crochet chain, crochet the next 3 stitches from the edge, repeat from * until no unworked stitches remain. Sew in ends and block. When blocking, pull each of the 13 peaks of the pattern to a point for the edging.

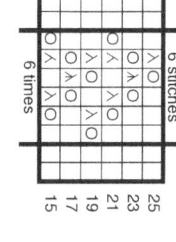
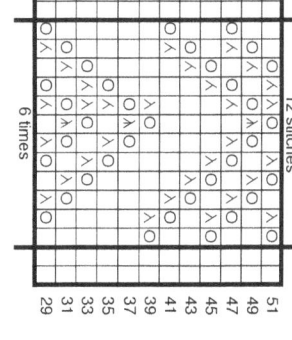
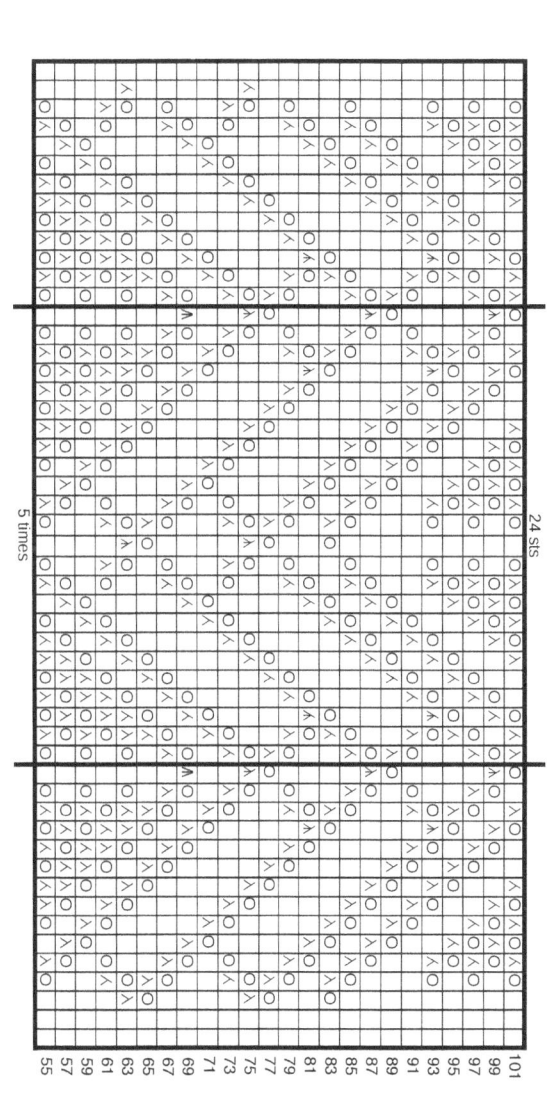
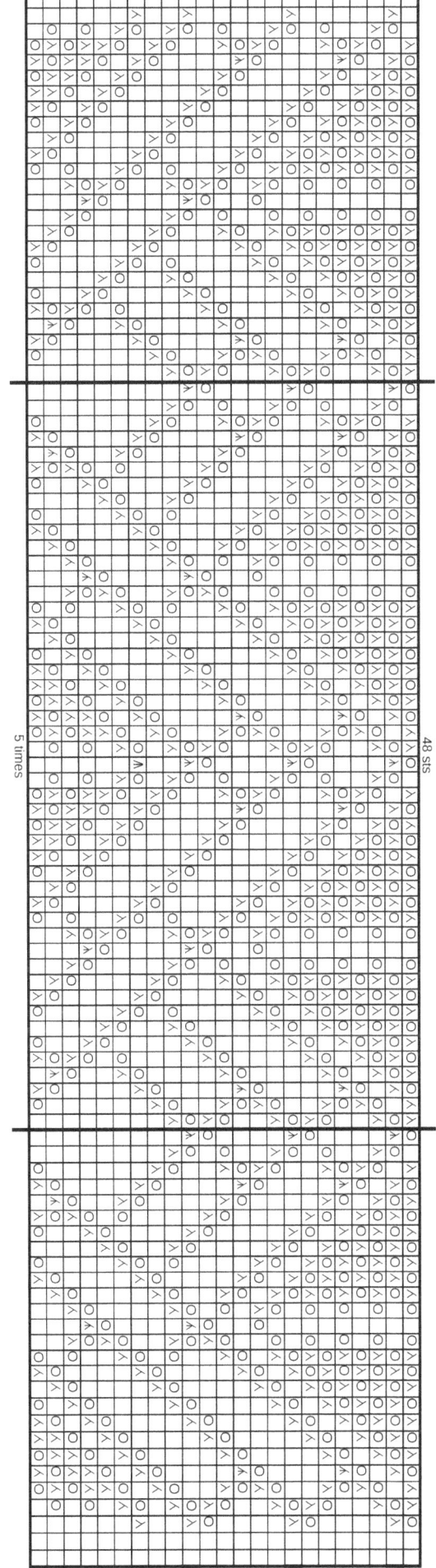

Zorya

(ADVENT KALENDAR 2015)

The Zorya are ancient Slavic sky and light goddesses. They are sisters; Utrennyaya, the morning star, and Vechernyaya, the evening star. Their purpose is to guard the doomsday hound Simargl who tries to eat Ursa Minor, the little bear. If the chain should ever break and the dog should ever get loose, the universe will end. The Zorya serve the sun god Dažbog. Zorya Utrennyaya opens the gates to his palace every morning for the sun-chariot's departure. At dusk, Zorya Vechernyaya closes the palace gates once more after his return.

Zorya

MATERIALS

Sample 1:
Pure 100% Merino Superwash from Wollmeise [100% Merino Superwash – 574 yds/525 m per 150 g]

1 skein *Herzblut* [C1] (actual usage: 382 yds/350 m, 100 g)

1 skein *Feldmaus* [C2] (actual usage: 325 yds/298 m, 85 g)

Sample 2:
Capri FS from Ashton Studio Arts [50% Merino, 50% silk – 430 yds/393 m per 100 g]

1 skein *Misty Dove* [C1]

1 skein *Purple Haze* [C2]

4.5 mm [US 7] needles

Stitch markers

Large-eyed, blunt needle

GAUGE

14 sts and 26 rows = 10 cm [4 in] in garter stitch, blocked

FINISHED (BLOCKED) SIZE

Wingspan: 175 cm (69 in), height: 74 cm (29 in)

INSTRUCTIONS

With [C1]: CO 4 sts

Row 1 (RS): K4.

Row 2: MP, k to the end.

Row 3: K2, M1, k2.

Row 4: K2tog, kfb, k2.

Row 5: K2, M1, k to the end.

Row 6: MP, k to the end.

Row 7: K2, M1, k to the end.

Row 8: K2tog, k until 3 sts rem, kfb, k2. (7 sts)

Work rows 5-8 SEVEN more times. (21 sts)

DAY 2

With [C2]:
Row 37: K2, M1, k to the end.

Row 38: MP, k to the end.

With [C1]:
Row 39: K2, M1, k to the end.

Row 40: K2tog, k until 3 sts rem, kfb, k2.

Work rows 37-40 FIVE more times. (33 sts)

DAY 3

With [C1]:
Row 61: K2, M1, k to the end.

Row 62: MP, k to the end.

Row 63: K2, M1, k to the end.

Row 64: K2tog, k until 3 sts rem, kfb, k2.

Work rows 61-64 TWO more times. (39 sts)

Row 73: K2, M1, k to the end.

Row 74: MP, k to the end.

With [C2]:
Row 75: K2, M1, k to the end.

Row 76: K2tog, k until 3 sts rem, kfb, k2.

With [C1]
Row 77: K2, M1, k to the end.

Row 78: MP, k to the end.

Row 79: K2, M1, k1, [yo, k2tog] 19 times, k1.

Row 80: K2tog, k until 3 sts rem, kfb, k2. (43 sts)

DAY 4

With [C2]:
Row 81: K2, M1, k to the end.

Row 82: MP, k to the end.

With [C1]:
Row 83: K2, M1, k to the end.

Row 84: K2tog, k until 3 sts rem, kfb, k2.

Row 85: K2, M1, k2, [yo, k2tog] 20 times, k1.

Row 86: MP, k to the end.

With [C2]:
Row 87: K2, M1, k to the end.

Row 88: K2tog, k until 3 sts rem, kfb, k2.

With [C1]:
Row 89: K2, M1, k to the end.

Row 90: MP, k to the end.

Row 91: K2, M1, k to the end.

Row 92: K2tog, k until 3 sts rem, kfb, k2. (49 sts)

DAY 5

With [C1]:
Row 93: K2, M1, k to the end.

Row 94: MP, k to the end.

Row 95: K2, M1, kto the end.

Row 96: K2tog, k until 3 sts rem, kfb, k2.

Row 97: K2, M1, k to the end.

Row 98: MP, k to the end.

With [C2]:
Row 99: K2, M1, k to the end.

Row 100: K2tog, k until 3 sts rem, kfb, k2.

With [C1]:
Row 101: K2, M1, k to the end.

Row 102: MP, k to the end.

Row 103: K2, M1, k1, [yo, k2tog] 25 times, k1.

Row 104: K2tog, k until 3 sts rem, kfb, k2. (55 sts)

DAY 6

With [C2]:
Row 105: K2, M1, k to the end.

Row 106: MP, k to the end.

With [C1]:
Row 107: K2, M1, k to the end.

Row 108: K2tog, k until 3 sts rem, kfb, k2.

Row 109: K2, M1, k to the end.

Row 110: MP, k to the end.

Work rows 107-110 ONE more time.

Rpw 115: K2, M1, k to the end.

Row 116: K2tog, k until 3 sts rem, kfb, k2. (61 sts)

DAY 7

With [C2]:
Row 117: K2, M1, k to the end.

Row 118: MP, k to the end.

With [C1]:
Row 119: K2, M1, k to the end.

Row 120: K2tog, k until 3 sts rem, kfb, k2.

Row 121: K2, M1, k1, [k2tog, yo, k1, yo, ssk, k1] 9 times, k2tog, yo, k4.

Row 122: MP, k4, [yo, CDD, yo, k3] 9 times, yo, k2tog, k3.

Row 123: K2, M1, k2, [yo, ssk, k1, k2tog, yo, k1] 9 times, yo, ssk, k4.

Row 124: K2tog, k1, ssk, yo, [k3, yo, CDD, yo] 9 times, k3, kfb, k2.

With [C2]:
Row 125: K2, M1, k to the end.

Row 126: MP, k to the end. (66 sts)

DAY 8

With [C2]:
Row 127: K2, M1, k to the end.

Row 128: K2tog, k until 3 sts rem, kfb, k2.

With [C1]:
Row 129: K2, M1, k to the end.

Row 130: MP, k to the end.

Row 131: K2, M1, k2, [k2tog, yo, k1, yo, ssk, k1] 10 times, k4.

Row 132: K2tog, k2, ssk, yo, [k3, yo, CDD, yo] 9 times, k3, yo, k2tog, k1, kfb, k2.

Row 133: K2, M1, k1, [k2tog, yo, k1, yo, ssk, k1] 10 times, k2tog, yo, k4.

Row 134: MP, k4, [yo, CDD, yo, k3] 10 times, yo, k2tog, k3. (70 sts)

DAY 9

With [C2]:
Row 135: K2, M1, k to the end.

Row 136: K2tog, k until 3 sts rem, kfb, k2.

With [C1]:
Row 137: K2, M1, k to the end.

Row 138: MP, k to the end.

Row 139: K2, M1, k to the end.

Row 140: K2tog, k until 3 sts rem, kfb, k2.

Work rows 137-140 ONE more time. (75 sts)

DAY 10

With [C1]:
Row 145: K2, M1, k to the end.

Row 146: MP, k to the end.

Row 147: K2, M1, k to the end.

Row 148: K2tog, k until 3 sts rem, kfb, k2

Work rows 145-148 TWO more times. (81 sts)

DAY 11

With [C2]:
Row 157: K2, M1, k to the end.

Row 158: MP, k to the end.

Row 159: K2, M1, k1, [k1, yo, ssk, k1, k2tog, yo] 12 times, k1, yo, ssk, k4.

Row 160: K2tog, k1, ssk, yo, [k3, yo, CDD, yo] 12 times, k3, kfb, k2.

Row 161: K2, M1, k1, [yo, ssk, k1, k2tog, yo, k1] 13 times, k2.

Row 162: MP, [k3, yo, CDD, yo] 13 times, k5.

Row 163: K2, M1, k2, [k2tog, yo, k1, yo, ssk, k1] 13 times, k2.

Row 164: K2tog, k2, [k3, yo, CDD, yo] 13 times, kfb, k2.

Row 165: K2, M1, [k1, k2tog, yo, k1, yo, ssk] 13 times, k1, k2tog, yo, k2.

Row 166: MP, k2, [yo, CDD, yo, k3] 13 times, yo, k2tog, kfb, k2.

Row 167: K2, M1, [k2tog, yo, k1, yo, ssk, k1] 13 times, k2tog, yo, k5.

Row 168: K2tog, k1, [k3, yo, CDD, yo] 13 times, k4, kfb, k2. (88 sts)

DAY 12

With [C2]:
Row 169: K2, M1, k2, [yo, ssk, k1, k2tog, yo, k1] 13 times, yo, ssk, k4.

Row 170: MP, k1, [yo, CDD, yo, k3] 14 times, k3.

Row 171: K2, M1, [yo, ssk, k1, k2tog, yo, k1] 14 times, k3.

Row 172: K2tog, [k3, yo, CDD, yo] 14 times, k4.

Row 173: K2, M1, [k1, k2tog, yo, k1, yo, ssk] 14 times, k3.

Row 174: MP, k1, ssk, yo, [k3, yo, CDD, yo] 13 times, k3, yo, k2tog, k3.

Row 175: K2, M1, k2, [yo, ssk, k1, k2tog, yo, k1] 14 times, k2.

Row 176: K2tog, k2, [yo, CDD, yo, k3] 14 times, kfb, k2.

Row 177: K2, M1, [k1, yo, ssk, k1, k2tog, yo] 14 times, k1, yo, ssk, k2.

Row 178: MP, ssk, yo, [k3, yo, CDD, yo] 14 times, k5. (92 sts)

DAY 13

With [C2]:
Row 179: K2, M1, k to the end.

Row 180: K2tog, k until 3 sts rem, kfb, k2.

With [C1]:
Row 181: K2, M1, k to the end.

Row 182: MP, k to the end.

Row 183: K2, M1, k to the end.

Row 184: K2tog, k until 3 sts rem, kfb, k2.

Work rows 181-184 TWO more times. (99 sts)

DAY 14

With [C1]:
Row 193: K2, M1, k to the end.

Row 194: MP, k to the end.

With [C2]:
Row 195: K2, M1, k to the end.

Row 196: K2tog, k until 3 sts rem, kfb, k2.

With [C1]:
Row 197: K2, M1, k to the end.

Row 198: MP, k to the end.

Row 199: K2, M1, [yo, k2tog] 49 times, k2.

Row 200: K2tog, k until 3 sts rem, kfb, k2.

With [C2]:
Row 201: K2, M1, k to the end.

Row 202: MP, k to the end. (104 sts)

DAY 15

With [C1]:
Row 203: K2, M1, k to the end.

Row 204: K2tog, k until 3 sts rem, kfb, k2.

Row 205: K2, M1, k to the end.

Row 206: MP, k to the end.

Work rows 203-206 TWO more times. (110 sts)

DAY 16

With [C1]:
Row 215: K2, M1, k to the end.

Row 216: K2tog, k until 3 sts rem, kfb, k2.

With [C2]:
Row 217: K2, M1, k to the end.

Row 218: MP, k to the end.

With [C1]:
Row 219: K2, M1, k to the end.

Row 220: K2tog, k until 3 sts rem, kfb, k2.

Row 221: K2, M1, k to the end.

Row 222: MP, k to the end.

With [C2]:
Row 223: K2, M1, k to the end.

Row 224: K2tog, k until 3 sts rem, kfb, k2.

With [C1]:
Row 225: K2, M1, k to the end.

Row 226: MP, k to the end.

Row 227: K2, M1, k to the end.

Row 228: K2tog, k until 3 sts rem, kfb, k2. (117 sts)

DAY 17

With [C2]:
Row 229: K2, M1, k to the end.

Row 230: MP, k to the end.

With [C1]:
Row 231: K2, M1, k to the end.

Row 232: K2tog, k until 3 sts rem, kfb, k2.

Row 233: K2, M1, k2, [yo, k2tog] 57 times, k1.

Row 234: MP, k to the end.

With [C2]:
Row 235: K2, M1, k to the end.

Row 236: K2tog, k until 3 sts rem, kfb, k2.

With [C1]:
Row 237: K2, M1, k to the end.

Row 238: MP, k to the end.

Row 239: K2, M1, k to the end.

Row 240: K2tog, k until 3 sts rem, kfb, k2. (123 sts)

DAY 18

With [C2]:
Row 241: K2, M1, k to the end.

Row 242: MP, k to the end.

With [C1]:
Row 243: K2, M1, k to the end.

Row 244: K2tog, k until 3 sts rem, kfb, k2.

Row 245: K2, M1, k to the end.

Row 246: MP, k to the end.

With [C2]:
Row 247: K2, M1, k to the end.

Row 248: K2tog, k until 3 sts rem, kfb, k2.

With [C1]:
Row 249: K2, M1, k to the end.

Row 250: MP, k to the end.

Row 251: K2, M1, [k1, k2tog, yo, k1, yo, ssk] 20 times, k1, k2tog, yo, k3.

Row 252: K2tog, k2, [yo, CDD, yo, k3] 20 times, yo, k2tog, kfb, k2. (129 sts)

DAY 19

With [C1]:
Row 253: K2, M1, [k2tog, yo, k1, yo, ssk, k1] 21 times, k1.

Row 254: MP, k2, [k3, yo, CDD, yo] 20 times, k3, yo, k2tog, k2.

Row 255: K2, M1, (k1, yo, ssk, k1, k2tog, yo) 20 times, k1, yo, ssk, k5.

Row 256: K2tog, k1, yo, CDD yo, [k3, yo, CDD, yo] 20 times, k2, kfb, k2.

Row 257: K2, M1, [yo, ssk, k1, k2tog, yo, k1] 21 times, k3.

Row 258: MP, k4, [yo, CDD, yo, k3] 21 times, k1.

Row 259: K2, M1, [k1, k2tog, yo, k1, yo, ssk] 21 times, k4.

Row 260: K2tog, k1, ssk, yo, [k3, yo, CDD, yo] 20 times, k3, yo, k2tog, kfb, k2. (133 sts)

DAY 20

With [C1]:
Row 261: K2, M1, [k2tog, yo, k1, yo, ssk, k1] 21 times, k2tog, yo, k3

Row 262: MP, [k3, yo, CDD, yo] 21 times, k3, yo, k2tog, k2.

Row 263: K2, M1, k to the end.

Row 264: K2tog, k until 3 sts rem, kfb, k2.

With [C2]:
Row 265: K2, M1, k to the end.

Row 266: MP, k to the end.

Row 267: K2, M1, k to the end.

Row 268: K2tog, k until 3 sts rem, kfb, k2.

Row 269: K2, M1, k to the end.

Row 270: MP, k to the end. (138 sts)

DAY 21

With [C2]:
Row 271: K2, M1, k to the end.

Row 272: K2tog, k until 3 sts rem, kfb, k2.

Row 273: K2, M1, k to the end.

Row 274: MP, k to the end.

Work rows 271-274 ONE more time.

Row 279: K2, M1, k to the end.

Row 280: K2tog, k until 3 sts rem, kfb, k2. (143 sts)

DAY 22

With [C1]:
Row 281: K2, M1, k to the end.

Row 282: MP, k to the end.

With [C2]:
Row 283: K2, M1, k to the end.

Row 284: K2tog, k until 3 sts rem, kfb, k2.

Row 285: K2, M1, k2, [yo, k2tog] 70 times, k1.

Row 286: MP, k to the end.

With [C1]:
Row 287: K2, M1, k to the end.

Row 288: K2tog, k until 3 sts rem, kfb, k2.

With [C2]:
Row 289: K2, M1, k to the end.

Row 290: MP, k to the end.

Row 291: K2, M1, k2, [yo, k2tog] 71 times, k2.

Row 292: K2tog, k until 3 sts rem, kfb, k2. (149 sts)

DAY 23

With [C1]:
Row 293: K2, M1, k to the end.

Row 294: MP, k to the end.
With [C2]

Row 295: K2, M1, k to the end.

Row 296: K2tog, k until 3 sts rem, kfb, k2.

Row 297: K2, M1, k to the end.

Row 298: MP, k to the end.

Work rows 295-298 ONE more time. (154 sts)

DAY 24

With [C2]:
Row 303: K2, M1, k to the end.

Row 304: K2tog, k until 3 sts rem, kfb, k2.

Row 305: K2, M1, k to the end.

Row 306: MP, k to the end. Work rows 303-306 TWO more times. (160 sts)

FINISHING INSTRUCTIONS

With [C2]:
Bind off as follows:

[CO2, k1, (k1, return 2 sts to ln, k2tog tbl) 6 times, return 1 st to ln] 39 times, CO2, k, (k1, return 2 sts to ln, k2tog tbl) until no unworked sts remain.

Sew in ends and block.

Dažbog

(ADVENT KALENDAR 2016)

Dažbog is the ancient Slavic sun god. He rides the sun-chariot across the sky every day, and gives light to the world. The sun has been forged by his father, Svarog.

Dažbog begins each day as an infant, and ends each day as an old man. At night, he travels through the underworld. As the light grows scarce at the winter solstice, we wish for the return of the sun, and call for Dažbog to once more begin to spend more time with us.

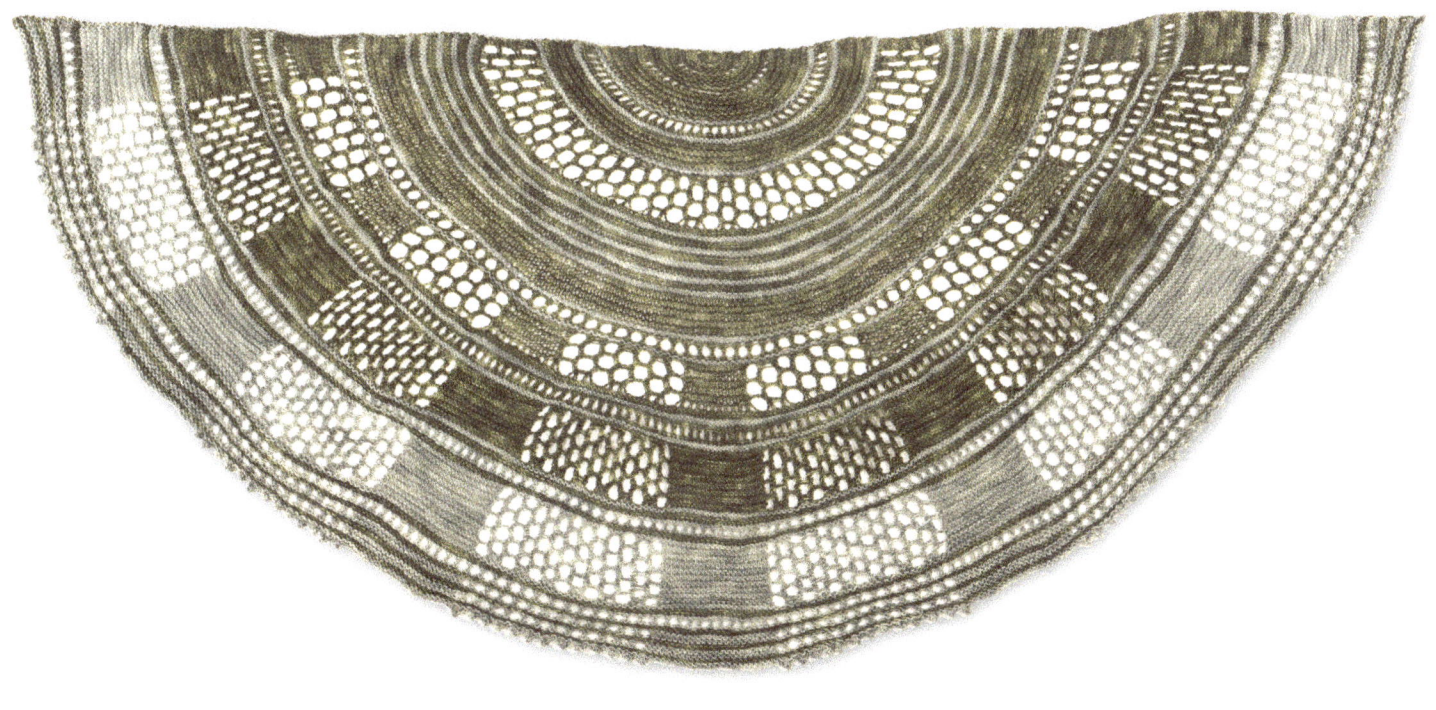

Dažbog

MATERIALS

Sample 1:

1 skein CaribouBaa from Indigodragonfly [100% Merino Superwash – 435 yds/398 meters per 100 g] in *Sage Fright* [C1]

1 skein CaribouBaa from Indigodragonfly [100% Merino Superwash – 435 yds/398 meters per 100 g] in *Antiques Freakshow* [C2]

Sample 2:

1 skein Cashmere Blend Fingering from Skeined Alive Yarns [80% Merino, 10% Nylon, 10% Cashmere – 435 yds/398 meters per 100 g] in *Vermiculture* [C1]

1 skein Dreamy from Anzula [75% Merino, 15% Cashmere, 10% Silk – 385 yds/352 meters per 114 g] in *Bark* [C2]

4.5 mm [US 7] needles

Stitch markers

Large-eyed, blunt needle

GAUGE

16 sts and 19 rows = 10 cm [4 in] in garter stitch, blocked

FINISHED (BLOCKED) SIZE

Wingspan: 170 cm (67 in), height: 85 cm (33.5 in)

INSTRUCTIONS

CO 3 sts using a provisional cast-on.

Setup Row 1-7: K3.

Setup Row 8: K3, pick up and knit 4 sts along the side of the knitting (one from each purl-bump), pick up and knit 3 sts from the provisional cast-on. (10 sts)

Setup Row 9: Knit.

Row 1 (RS): K3, yo, [k1, yo] 4 times, k3. (15 sts0

Row 2: K3, [ktbl, k1] 4 times, ktbl, k3.

Row 3-4: Knit.

Row 5: K3, [k1, yo] 9 times, k3. (24 sts)

Row 6: K3, [ktbl, k1] 9 times, k3.

Row 7-12: Knit

Row 13: K3, [k1, yo] 18 times, k3. (42 sts)

Row 14: K3, [ktbl, k1] 18 times, k3.

From this point on, instructions are both written and charted. Work the white rows in C1 and the shaded gray rows with C2.

Row 15-22: Knit.

With [C2]:
Row 23-24: Knit.

With [C1]:
Row 25-26: Knit.

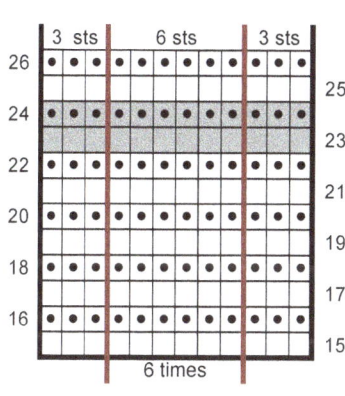

DAY 2

Row 27: K3, [yo, k1] 36 times, yo, k3. (79 sts)

Row 28: Knit.

With [C2]:
Row 29-30: Knit.

With [C1]:
Row 31-38: Knit.

With [C2]:
Row 39-40: Knit.

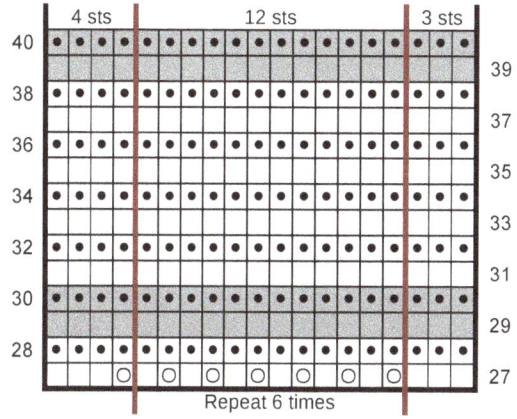

DAY 3

With [C1]:
Row 41-42: Knit.

Row 43: K3, yo, [yo, k4, yo] 18 times, yo, k4.

Row 44: K2, k2tog, k1, [p1, k2tog, k2tog, k1] 18 times, p1, k2tog, k1.

Row 45: K3, [k2, yo, yo, k2] 18 times, k4.

Row 46: K4, [k2tog, k1, p1, k2tog] 18 times, k3.

Rows 47-50: As rows 43-46.

Rows 51-52: As rows 43-44.

DAY 4

Row 53: K4, [yo, k1] 72 times, k3. (151 sts)

Row 54: K3, [k1, ktbl] 72 times, k4.

With [C2]:
Row 55-56: Knit.

With [C1]:
Row 57-58: Knit.

With [C2]:
Row 59-60: Knit.

With [C1]:
Row 61-62: Knit.

DAY 5

With [C2]:
Row 63-64: Knit.

With [C1]:
Row 65-66: Knit.

With [C2]:
Row 67-68: Knit.

With [C1]:
Row 69-70: Knit.

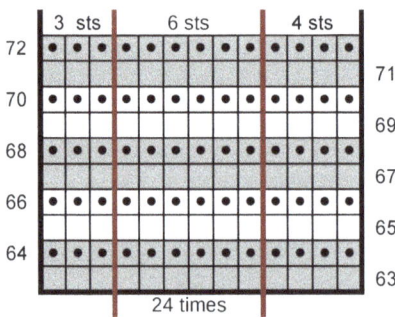

With [C2]:
Row 71-72: Knit.

DAY 6

With [C1]:
Row 73-82: Knit.

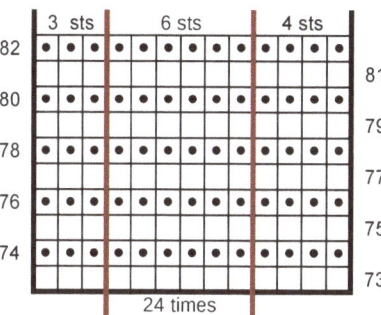

DAY 7

With [C2]:
Row 83-84: Knit.

With [C1]:
Row 85-86: Knit.

Row 87: K4, [yo, k2tog] 72 times, k3.

Row 88: Knit.

With [C2]:
Row 89-90: Knit.

With [C1]:
Row 91-92: Knit.

DAY 8

Row 93: K4, [k6, yo, yo, k4, yo, yo, k4, yo, yo, k4, yo yo, k6] 6 times, k3.

Row 94: K3, [k4, k2tog, k1, p1, k2tog, k2tog, k1, p1, k2tog, k2tog, k1, p1, k2tog, k2tog, k1, p1, k2tog, k4] 6 times, k4.

Row 95: K4, [k8, yo, yo, k4, yo, yo, k4, yo, yo, k8] 6 times, k3.

Row 96: K3, [k6, k2tog, k1, p1, k2tog, k2tog, k1, p1, k2tog, k2tog, k1, p1, k2tog, k6] 6 times, k4.

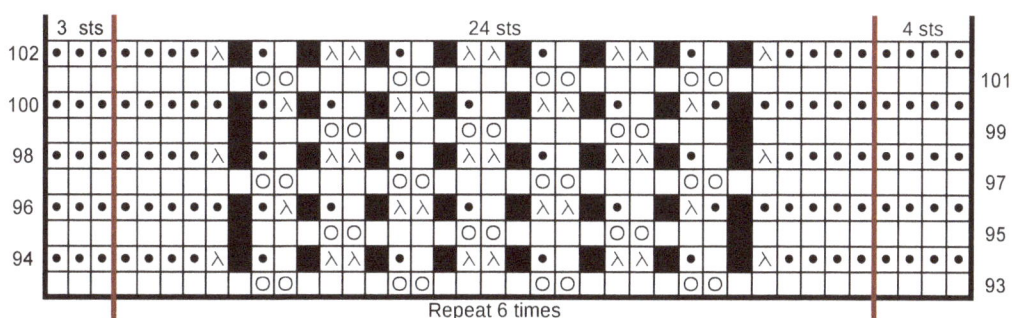

Rows 97-100: As rows 93-96.

Rows 101-102: As rows 93-94.

DAY 9

Row 103: K4, [yo, k1] 144 times, k3. [295 sts]

Row 104: K3, [k1, ktbl] 144 times, k4.

With [C2]:
Row 105-106: Knit.

With [C1]:
Row 107-108: Knit.

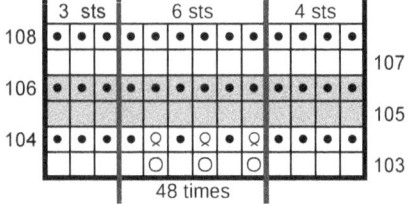

DAY 10

Row 109: K3, yo, [k2tog, yo] 144 times, k2tog, k2.

Row 110: Knit.

With [C2]:
Rows 111-112: Knit.

With [C1]:
Rows 113-114: Knit.

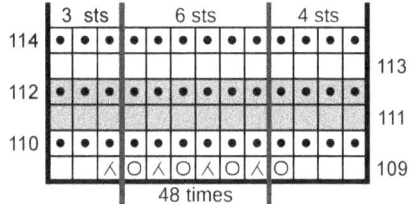

DAY 11

Row 115: K4, [k13, yo, (yo, k4, yo) 6 times, yo, k11] 6 times, k3.

Row 116: K3, [k9, k2tog, k1, (p1, k2tog, k2tog, k1) 6 times, p1, k2tog, k11] 6 times, k4.

Row 117: K4, [k13, (k2, yo, yo, k2) 6 times, k11] 6 times, k3.

Row 118: K3, [k11, (k2tog, k1, p1, k2tog) 6 times, k13] 6 times, k4.

Row 119-120: As rows 115-116.

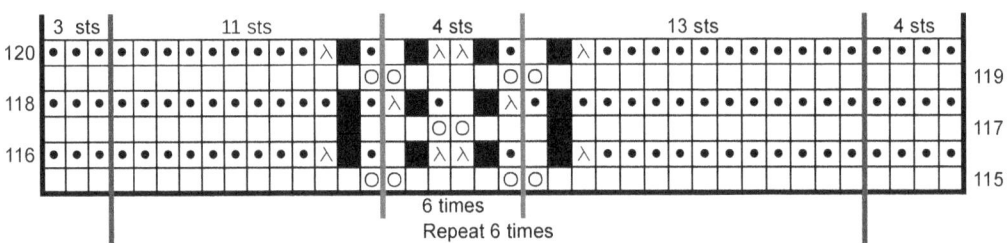

DAY 12

Row 121: K4, [k13, (k2, yo, yo, k2) 6 times, k11] 6 times, k3.

Row 122: K3, [k11, (k2tog, k1, p1, k2tog) 6 times, k13] 6 times, k4.

Row 123: K4, [k13, yo, (yo, k4, yo) 6 times, yo, k11] 6 times, k3.

Row 124: K3, [k9, k2tog, k1, (p1, k2tog, k2tog, k1) 6 times, p1, k2tog, k11] 6 times, k4.

Rows 125-126: As rows 121-122.

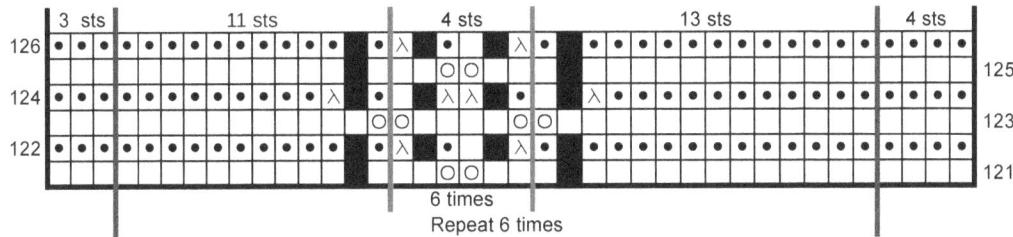

DAY 13

Row 127: K4, [k13, yo, (yo, k4, yo) 6 times, yo, k11] 6 times, k3.

Row 128: K3, [k9, k2tog, k1, (p1, k2tog, k2tog, k1) 6 times, p1, k2tog, k11] 6 times, k4.

With [C2]:
Rows 129-130: Knit.

With [C1]:
Rows 131-132: Knit.

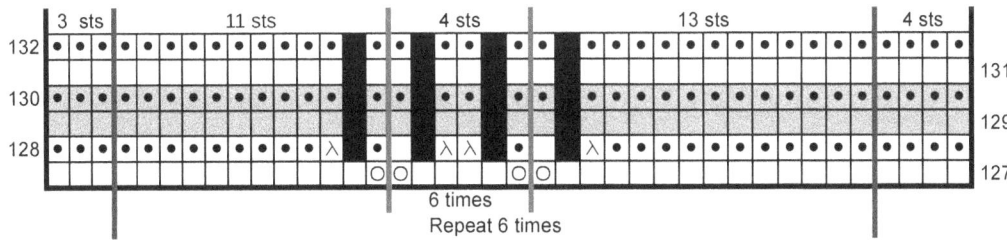

DAY 14

With [C2]:
Row 133-134: Knit.

Row 135: K4, [k2tog, yo] 144 times, k3.

Row 136: Knit.

With [C1]:
Rows 137-138: Knit.

DAY 15

With [C2]:
Rows 139-140: Knit.

Row 141: K4, [k13, yo, (yo, k4, yo) 6 times, yo, k11] 6 times, k3.

Row 142: K3, [k9, k2tog, k1, (p1, k2tog, k2tog, k1) 6 times, p1, k2tog, k11] 6 times, k4.

Row 143: K4, [k13, (k2, yo, yo, k2) 6 times, k11] 6 times, k3.

Row 144: K3, [k11, (k2tog, k1, p1, k2tog) 6 times, k13] 6 times, k4.

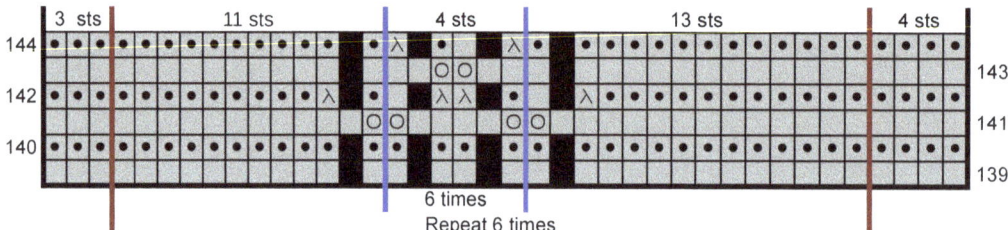

DAY 16

Row 145: K4, [k13, yo, (yo, k4, yo) 6 times, yo, k11] 6 times, k3.

Row 146: K3, [k9, k2tog, k1, (p1, k2tog, k2tog, k1) 6 times, p1, k2tog, k11] 6 times, k4.

Row 147: K4, [k13, (k2, yo, yo, k2) 6 times, k11] 6 times, k3.

Row 148: K3, [k11, (k2tog, k1, p1, k2tog) 6 times, k13] 6 times, k4.

Rows 149-150: As rows 145-146.

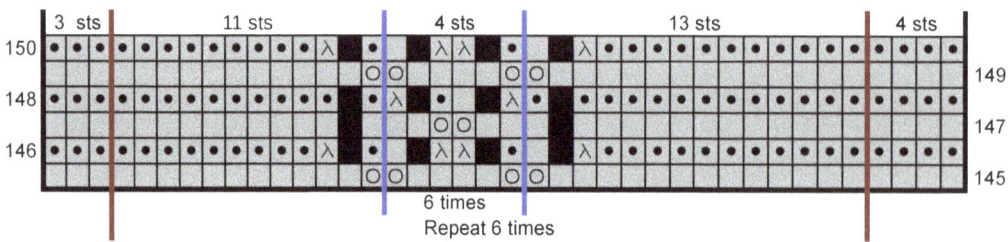

DAY 17

Row 151: K4, [k13, (k2, yo, yo, k2) 6 times, k11] 6 times, k3.

Row 152: K3, [k11, (k2tog, k1, p1, k2tog) 6 times, k13] 6 times, k4.

Row 153: K4, [k13, yo, (yo, k4, yo) 6 times, yo, k11] 6 times, k3.

Row 154: K3, [k9, k2tog, k1, (p1, k2tog, k2tog, k1) 6 times, p1, k2tog, k11] 6 times, k4.

Rows 155-156: As rows 151-152.

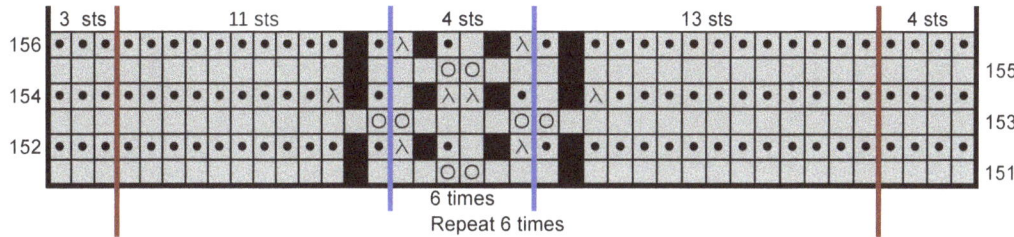

DAY 18

Row 157: K4, [k13, yo, (yo, k4, yo) 6 times, yo, k11] 6 times, k3.

Row 158: K3, [k9, k2tog, k1, (p1, k2tog, k2tog, k1) 6 times, p1, k2tog, k11] 6 times, k4.

Rows 159-160: Knit.

With [C1]:
Rows 161-162: Knit.

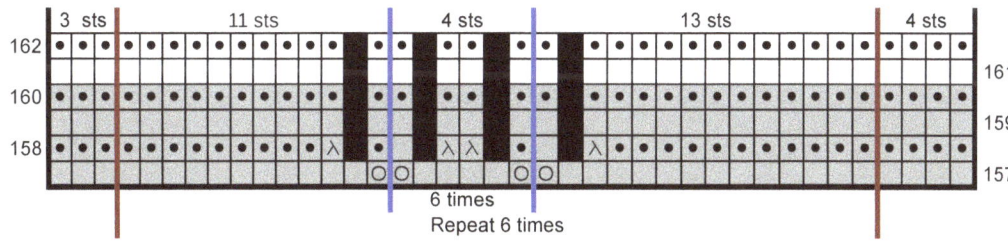

DAY 19

With [C2]:
Rows 163-164: Knit.

Row 165: K3, yo, [k2tog, yo] 144 times, k2tog, k2.

Row 166: Knit.

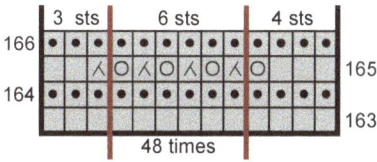

DAY 20

With [C1]:
Rows 167-168: Knit.

With [C2]:
Rows 169-170: Knit.

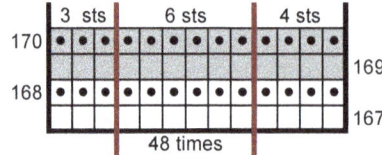

DAY 21

Row 171: K4, [k13, (yo, k2tog) 13 times, k9] 6 times, k3.

Row 172: Knit.

With [C1]:
Rows 173-174: Knit.

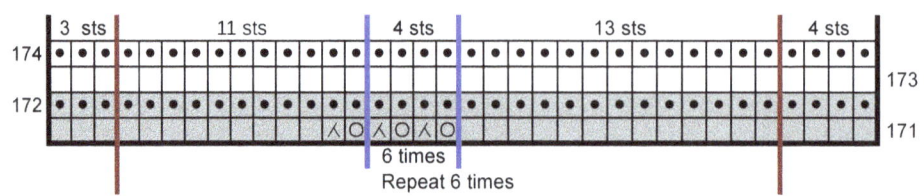

DAY 22

With [C2]:
Rows 175-176: Knit.

Row 177: K4, [k13, (yo, k2tog) 13 times, k9] 6 times, k3.

Row 178: Knit.

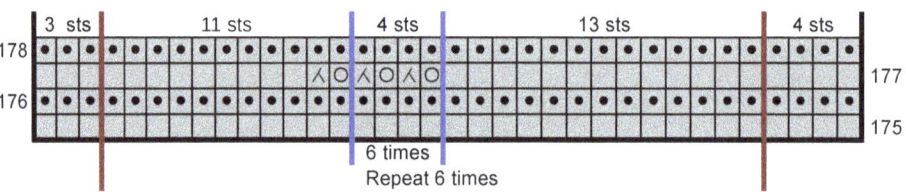

DAY 23

With [C1]:
Rows 179-180: Knit.

With [C2]:
Rows 181-182: Knit.

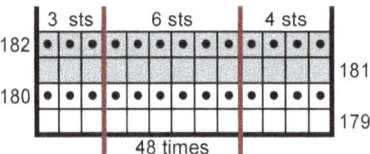

DAY 24

Optional: If you would like to make the shawl larger, repeat rows 177-182 up to three times more.

FINISHING INSTRUCTIONS

With [C2]:
Bind off as follows: K1, (k1, return 2 sts to ln, k2tog tbl) 4 times, {(k1, return 2 sts to ln, k2tog tbl) 12 times, [return 1 st to ln, CO2, k1, (k1, return 2 sts to ln, k2tog tbl) 4 times] 13 times, (k1, return 2 sts to ln, k2tog tbl) 10 times} 6 times, (k1, return 2 sts to ln, k2tog tbl) until no unworked sts remain.

Sew in ends and block.

Abbreviations

BO – bind off

cn – cable needle

C1, C2 – color 1, color 2 etc (for gradient kits, 1-5 goes lightest to darkest)

CDD – centered double decrease: slip 2 stitches together (knitwise), k, psso

CO – cast on

k – knit

kfb – knit in the front and the back of the stitch

ktbl – knit through the back loop

k2tog – knit 2 stitches together

k3tog – knit 3 stitches together

ln – left needle

M1 – make one

MP – make picot: CO2, k2, return 2 sts to ln, k2tog tbl, k1, return 2 sts to ln, k2tog tbl

nupp – [K, yo] 3 times, k all into the same stitch.

Note: All 7 nupp stitches either knit together through the back loop on the subsequent rnd on a circular shawl, or purled together through the back loop on the subsequent row on a semi-circular shawl.

p – purl

PM – place marker

ptbl – purl through the back loop

psso – pass slipped stitch(es) over

p2tog – purl 2 stitches together

p3tog – purl 3 stitches together

rep – repeat

RM – remove marker

rn – right needle

rnd – round

RS – right side

SC1, SC2 – the 2 colors if using two contrasting colors

sl – slip

SM – slip marker

ssk – slip stitch as if to knit, slip stitch as if to knit, replace on left needle and knit both stitches together through the back loop

sssk – slip stitch as if to knit, slip stitch as if to knit, slip stitch as if to knit, replace on left needle and knit all three stitches together through the back loop

st(s) – stitch(es)

WS – wrong side

yo – yarn over

Techniques

Invisible loop cast on: http://techknitting.blogspot.com/2007/02/casting-on-from-middle-disappearing.html for tutorial

Symbol Guide & Special Symbols

- □ k on RS, p on WS
- • p on RS, k on WS
- ktbl on RS, ptbl on WS
- k2tog
- k3tog
- ssk
- sl1, k2tog, psso
- CDD
- nupp
- O yarn over
- ■ no stitch
- BO
- − sl1
- M1
- V kfb

Mystic Supernova

- sssk
- CIRCULAR SHAWL: start rnd 1 st early, then work λ
- CIRCULAR SHAWL: start rnd 1 st early, then work ⋏
- SEMI-CIRCULAR SHAWL: replace with a ssk in the first repeat. At the end of the row, instead of finishing with k2 as usual, finish with k2tog, k.
- SEMI-CIRCULAR SHAWL: replace with a k2tog in the first repeat. And at the end of the row, instead of finishing with k2 as usual, finish with ssk, k.
- EDGING: k2tog last st of the edging with next st on body of the shawl

Mystic Ocean

- k2tog on RS, p2tog on WS
- ssk on rs, ssp on ws
- work 3 sts as follows: insert rn into 3rd st on ln and pass over previous 2 sts, then ktbl, yo, ktbl

Mystic Vortex

- k2tog last st of the edging with next st on body of the shawl
- CIRCULAR SHAWL: start rnd 1 st early, then work λ

Mystic Cuppa

- work 3 sts as follows: insert rn into 3rd st on ln and pass over previous 2 sts, then k, yo, k
- sl 1 st onto cn and hold in front of work, k2 from left needle, k from cn
- sl 2 sts onto cn and hold at back of work, k1 from left needle, k2 from cn
- sl 1 st onto cn1 and hold at front of work, sl 3 sts onto cn2 and hold at back of work, k1 from ln, k3 from cn2, k1 from cn1
- sl3 sts onto cn 1 and hold at front of work, sl 1 st onto cn2 and hold at back of work, k3 from ln, p1 from cn2, k3 from cn1

Mystic Cabin

- k2tog on RS, ssk on WS
- ssk on RS, k2tog on WS

Special Symbols (continued)

Mystic Junction

△ p2tog

△ ssp

△ p3tog

Mystic Sea Witch

△ CIRCULAR SHAWL: start rnd 1 st early, then work λ

△ CIRCULAR SHAWL: start rnd 1st early, then work ⋏

△ SEMI-CIRCULAR SHAWL: replace with a ssk in the rst repeat. At the end of the row, instead of finishing with k2 as usual, finish with k2tog, k

△ SEMI-CIRCULAR SHAWL: replace with a k2tog in the rst repeat. And at the end of the row, instead of finishing with k2 as usual, finish with ssk, k.

Mystic Haven

λ ssk on RS, k2tog on WS

Mystic Sunset

Aster – make 5 sts from 5 as follows: (sl1 and drop 1 from ky) 5 times, return to ln, then purl 5 sts tog, yo, p the same 5 sts tog, yo, p the same 5 sts

ky – knit but wrap the yarn around the needle twice

Mystic Mist

△ CIRCULAR SHAWL: start rnd 1 st early, then work λ

⋏ CIRCULAR SHAWL: start rnd 1 st early, then work ⋏

About Anna

Anna Dalvi grew up on the west coast of Sweden, but has lived in Ottawa, Canada for many years now. Anna holds a B.S. in Computer Science from Cornell University, and an M.B.A. from Queen's University.

Anna has been publishing knitting patterns online since 2007. Her most popular designs are the Mystic lace shawls, originally published in a mystery knitalong format, which have attracted many thousands of knitters worldwide.

She is the author of Shaping Shawls (2011), Ancient Egypt in Lace and Color (2012), Fairy Tale Lace (2013), Mystic Shawls (2014), Reversible Lace (2017), and Seven Fingerless Mittens (2011). Her work has also been featured in several other publications and magazines.

In her knitting, Anna enjoys variety more than anything else—from intricate lace to sprawling cables, and differences in color and texture. Her inspiration comes from nature, music, fairy tales and myths.

About Cooperative Press

Cooperative Press (formerly anezka media) was founded in 2007 by Shannon Okey, a voracious reader as well as writer and editor, who had been doing freelance acquisitions work, introducing authors with projects she believed in to editors at various publishers. Although working with traditional publishers can be very rewarding, there are some books that fly under their radar. They're too avant-garde, or the marketing department doesn't know how to sell them, or they don't think they'll sell 50,000 copies in a year.

5,000 or 50,000. Does the book matter to that 5,000? Then it should be published.

In 2009, Cooperative Press (cooperativepress.com) changed its named to reflect the relationships we have developed with authors working on books. We work together to put out the best quality books we can and share in the proceeds accordingly.

Thank you for supporting independent publishers and authors.

ALSO FROM ANNA DALVI AND COOPERATIVE PRESS

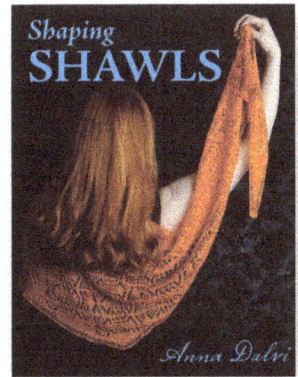

www.ingramcontent.com/pod-product-compliance
Lightning Source LLC
Chambersburg PA
CBHW051550220426
43671CB00024B/2994